Slow Cookin' in the Fast Lane

Julie Kay

Copy Editing
Camille M. Jeansonne

Cover Design and Art
Holly Kay

Photography
John Boss

COPYRIGHT 2001
by
Fast Lane Productions, L.L.C.

ISBN 0-9710782-0-3
Library of Congress Control Number 2001090126

To order additional copies of *Slow Cookin' in the Fast Lane,*
an order form is provided at the back of the book or write:

Fast Lane Productions, L.L.C.
P.O. Box 87527
Baton Rouge, LA 70879-8527

| First Printing | September 2001 | 5,000 copies |
| Second Printing | April 2002 | 5,000 copies |

WIMMER
COOKBOOKS
ConsolidatedGraphics
1-800-548-2537

TABLE OF CONTENTS

Acknowledgments

"Slow Cookin' in the Fast Lane" is the product of a dream nudged into reality -- some might say pushed and shoved was more like it. I always knew there was a market for more books on slow cooking that took into account the needs of busy moms, caregivers, professionals, singles, the retired -- just about any cook anywhere, but it took a lot of wonderful people to convince me that I could do this.

For their vision and their assistance in making a dream come true, I thank them, with special acknowledgment to Colette Dean.

To my family -- my husband, Bob, and my children, Holly and Jason -- who have alternately tried, criticized, praised, but nearly always supported my endeavors, what can I say? You are the best of the best.

I can't thank the readers of my newspaper column enough. "What a Crock!," published weekly in the Food section of the Baton Rouge, Louisiana, newspaper, The Advocate, has many dedicated readers who keep the column alive with their tips, recipes, and most of all, their encouragement.

Last, but not least, I acknowledge with much gratitude, the Advocate management and Food staff, including the editing expertise of Camille M. Jeansonne and the support of Food editor Tommy Simmons.

Introduction

Slow cookers have been in our home kitchens for more than 30 years now, and they have certainly changed with the times. In their original shades of avocado green, burnt orange, and harvest gold, Rival sold millions of the original slow cookers, known by their Crock-Pot ® trademark name. Today, they remain a popular item on wedding registries throughout the country, and the three original colors have given way to chrome and black, white, and a variety of modern, colorful flower and garden designs.

West Bend, Corningware, Hamilton Beach/Proctor-Silex, and Farberware have their own slow cookers on the market, and shapes are no longer just round. Removable stoneware inserts are now offered in an oval shape, most commonly from 3 1/2- to 6-quart size. The removable feature allows modern cooks the ease of cleaning they have come to not only expect, but demand.

Insulated carriers mean that transportation is easier than ever if you need to take a prepared dish to a family reunion, shower, or progressive dinner.

The slow cooker makes a convenient vehicle for cooks on the fast track who want to put a meal on their table at the end of some very long days. Professionals find the appliance an advantageous option for home cooking on the nutritious side.

Family schedules today run in so many different directions, from the baseball field to a ballet or piano lesson, and a multitude of after-school events, it's no wonder family cooks are stressed to the max.

To that end, a little extra time in the morning means your meal waits for you at the end of the day. If you have a family like mine, sometimes that means eating in shifts when a daughter shows up from college and your son has a late tennis practice. Dinner is not only ready when you are, but your home is filled with the delectable aroma of a home-cooked meal.

Most often, no stirring is required, and flavors have a chance to meld for maximum taste and moisture. Kitchen heat is reduced, and energy efficiency is a major advantage.

Within this book, you will find easy to follow recipes

complete with tips and a clock beside each list of ingredients. No recipe requires more than an estimated 15 minutes of preparation. You will also find a short glossary below that explains certain terms and ingredients found throughout the book that you may not be familiar with in your area:

Andouille -- A spicy, heavily smoked sausage often used in Cajun dishes. You may substitute smoked sausage if you are unable to locate andouille.

Lagniappe -- A little something extra.

Tasso -- A cured piece of pork or beef highly seasoned with a variety of seasonings and smoked for several days.

Tony Chachere's Original Seasoning -- A Creole seasoning mix found in a shaker-type container, often located on or near spice shelves.

Some of the most commonly asked questions regarding slow cooking include the following:

- *What is the temperature range when cooking on Low or High?* Low temps are around 200 degrees F. High is in the 300- to 350-degree F. range. Cooks wishing to speed cooking along can cook on High for a couple of hours, and then turn the temperature setting down to Low. Remember, every hour on High is equal to two hours on Low.

- *How much can I put in my slow cooker?* As a general rule, do not fill your cooker more than two-thirds full in order for food to cook properly. Check the manufacturer's instructions for exact specifications.

- *Is there an order in which foods should be placed into the stoneware insert?* Vegetables, such as potatoes, onions, and carrots, should be on the bottom, forming a rack for poultry or meat.

- *What about dairy products?* Dairy products in the slow cooker should be kept to a minimum because of a tendency for them to curdle when cooking over long periods of time. If you need to use products like sour cream or heavy cream, do so in the last hour or two of cooking.

- *What should I do when converting my recipes to slow cooking?* The good news is that many recipes can easily be converted from oven to slow cooking. The main thing is to watch the amount of liquid. Too many liquid ingredients can make a dish too soupy, so judge accordingly. You may also choose to increase the amount of seasonings to maximize flavor. A general rule to follow with regard to cooking time is if your recipe calls for an hour of baking time, the translation in slow cooking would be approximately 8 hours.

- *My slow cooker has an auto-shift feature. What does it do?* The auto-shift feature allows cooks to cook on High for an hour before automatically shifting down to Low. What this does is jump start the slow cooker to a higher temperature at the beginning of cooking time, which some cooks prefer for poultry or items that are especially cold.

- *Can I open the lid and peek?* Remember, lifting the lid can cause a loss of cooking time. Some experts say as much as 30 minutes are lost each time you lift the lid. If you need to stir the dish, do so, but only when called for in the recipe.

- *What about browning?* Some people like to brown meats before placing in the slow cooker. For seasoned roasts and pork chops, searing the meats may seal in the flavors and produce that crusty, baked look preferred by some cooks. As a rule, it is not necessary to brown meats, but for maximum flavor, I always brown meats, such as ground beef or ground turkey.

- *Can I put frozen meats in my slow cooker?* The USDA recommends that all meats and poultry be thawed before placing in the slow cooker.

- *Is slow cooking the same as Crock-Pot® cooking?* People often ask what's the difference? Rival, now part of the Holmes Group, holds the registered trademark for the name, "Crock-Pot®." That is why we refer to the process as slow cooking and other cookers as slow cookers.

- *What about cooking dried beans in my slow cooker?* Most often, dried beans benefit from soaking overnight before placing them in the slow cooker. Soak in enough water to cover beans and drain off water the next morning. Lentils do not need to soak overnight.

- *What size slow cooker do I need?* A family of four to six benefits from cookers in the 5- to 6-quart range, while singles and couples will do fine with the 3 1/2- to 4-quart models. Oval or round is your preference.

Most recipes in this book can be prepared in a 3 1/2- to 4-quart slow cooker, unless indicated in the recipe.

Here is a list of several major slow-cooker manufacturers if you need additional information:

- The Holmes Group (Rival Crock-Pots®)
  508-634-8050 or 800-546-5637

- General Electric
  877-207-0923

- Hamilton Beach/Proctor-Silex
  800-851-8900
  www.hamiltonbeach.com

- West Bend
  262-334-6949
  www.westbend.com

- Farberware
  800-233-9054
  www.farberware-electric@saltonusa.com

- Corningware
  800-557-9463

USDA FOOD SAFETY TIPS FOR SLOW COOKERS

The slow cooker, a counter-top appliance, cooks foods slowly at a low temperature, generally between 170 and 280 degrees F. The low heat helps less expensive, leaner cuts of meat become tender and shrink less. The direct heat from the pot, lengthy cooking time, and steam created within the tightly covered container combine to destroy bacteria and make the slow cooker a safe process for cooking foods.

Begin with a clean cooker, clean utensils, and a clean work area. Wash hands before and during food preparation.

Keep perishable foods refrigerated until preparation time. If you cut up meat and vegetables in advance, store them separately in the refrigerator. The slow cooker may take several hours to reach a safe, bacteria-killing temperature. Constant refrigeration assures that bacteria which multiply rapidly at room temperature won't get a "head start" during the first few hours of cooking.

Always defrost meat or poultry before putting it into a slow cooker.

Fill cooker no less than half full and no more than two-thirds full. Vegetables cook slower than meat and poultry in a slow cooker, so if using them, put vegetables in first, at the bottom and around sides of the stoneware insert. Then add meat and cover the food with liquid, such as broth, water, or barbecue sauce. Keep the lid in place, removing only to stir the food or check for doneness.

Most cookers have at least two settings. Certainly, foods will cook faster on High than on Low. However, for all-day cooking or for less-tender cuts, you may want to use the Low setting.

If possible, turn the cooker on the highest setting for the first hour of cooking time and then to Low, or the setting called for in your recipe. However, it's safe to cook foods on Low the entire time, if you're leaving for work, for example, and preparation time is limited. While food is cooking and once it's done, food will stay safe as long as the cooker is operating at its lowest setting.

If you are not at home during the entire slow-cooking process and the power goes out, THROW AWAY the food even if it looks done.

If you are at home, finish cooking the ingredients immediately by some other means, such as on a gas stove, on the outdoor grill, or at a friend's house where the power is on.

When you are at home, and if the food was completely cooked before the power went out, the food should remain safe up to two hours in the cooker with the power off.

Store leftovers in shallow, covered containers and refrigerate within two hours after cooking is finished. Reheating leftovers in a slow cooker is not recommended. However, cooked food can be brought to steaming on the stove top or in a microwave oven and then put into a preheated slow cooker to keep hot for serving.

Source: Information furnished by the Food Safety and Inspection Service, United States Department of Agriculture.

JILL'S CHICKEN

This is a wonderful comfort food recipe with a twist -- Cajun seasoning. It's become a favorite with our family.

1 whole fryer chicken or 8 chicken pieces
1/4 cup Tony Chachere's Original Seasoning
1/4 cup butter or margarine, sliced

1. Place chicken into slow cooker and sprinkle with seasoning.
2. Dot with slices of butter or margarine and cook on Low for 8 hours.
3. Serve with rice.

Serves 4 to 6.
Jill Arbour

The chicken will be falling-off-the-bone tender. Save leftovers for use in chicken salad sandwiches the next day.

CHICKEN SPAGHETTI

You could fill books with spaghetti recipes alone. Try this for a different version.

2 lbs. boneless, skinless chicken breasts or thighs
1 (1.5-oz.) packet dry spaghetti mix
2 cloves garlic, minced
2 onions, chopped
1 (14.5-oz.) can crushed tomatoes
1 (8-oz.) can tomato sauce
1 (6-oz.) can tomato paste
1 tbl. crushed red pepper flakes
1/2 tsp. Italian seasoning
1/2 tsp. black pepper
1/2 tsp. ground oregano
1 (16-oz.) package angel hair pasta
1 (8-oz.) package shredded mozzarella cheese

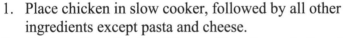

1. Place chicken in slow cooker, followed by all other ingredients except pasta and cheese.
2. Cook on Low for 6 to 8 hours. Near the end of cooking time, break up chicken into small pieces and stir.
3. Serve over angel hair pasta and sprinkle with mozzarella cheese.

Serves 6 to 8.

Leave a little time when you get home to cook the pasta, toss a salad, perhaps bake some garlic bread, and the meal is ready.

PARMESAN CHICKEN

For family members who don't like leftovers, this is a two-for-one meal that turns leftovers into something completely different.

1 whole fryer chicken or 8 chicken pieces
1 (1-lb.) jar Ragu Roasted Garlic
  Parmesan sauce
Cracked black pepper

5 MIN.

1. Place chicken into slow cooker. Sprinkle cracked black pepper generously over chicken and pour half of the Parmesan sauce over all.
2. Cook on High for 4 hours or on Low for 8 hours. One hour before completion of cooking time, pour the other half of Parmesan sauce over chicken. Serve over pasta.
3. Refrigerate any leftovers. The next day, shred chicken and mix with mayonnaise to the consistency you like. Add 1/4 cup of chopped grapes and sliced almonds to taste. Season with salt and pepper if desired and serve on croissant rolls or sandwich bread.

Serves 4 to 6.

Don't put the whole jar of sauce on your chicken at the beginning of roasting time. Save half in the refrigerator and an hour before completion, add the rest. It results in a more intense flavor.

GARLIC-MUSHROOM CHICKEN

Look at the number of convenience products available to help time-starved families with their meal dilemmas. Try a few.

1 whole fryer chicken or 8 chicken pieces
1 (2.1-oz.) packet Recipe Secrets/Garlic Mushroom flavor
** soup mix**
2 tbls. olive oil
8 ozs. fresh mushrooms, sliced
1 medium onion, sliced
3 garlic cloves, minced
1 (16-oz.) package fresh baby carrots

1. Rub olive oil over whole chicken and coat with garlic mushroom seasoning packet.
2. Place in slow cooker and position fresh mushrooms, onion, garlic, and carrots along the sides of the cooker.
3. Cook on Low for 6 to 8 hours.

Serves 4 to 6.

You may also use boneless, skinless chicken pieces if you desire.

ARTICHOKE CHICKEN

Artichokes and chicken make a wonderful combination.

1 1/2 lbs. boneless, skinless chicken breasts
1 (8-oz.) package fresh mushrooms, sliced
2 (6-oz.) jars marinated artichoke hearts, drained
4 cloves garlic, minced
1/4 cup white wine
2 tsps. black pepper
Angel hair pasta

1. Place chicken, mushrooms, and artichoke hearts in slow cooker. Add in garlic, white wine, and black pepper.
2. Cook on Low for 6 to 8 hours. Prepare angel hair pasta and, using a slotted spoon, place slow-cooked mixture over pasta. Use a ladle to spoon sauce over all.

Serves 4 to 6.

 If you wish to leave out the white wine, do not drain the marinated artichokes. Allow the marinade liquid to blend with the other ingredients.

BLUE CHEESE CHICKEN

The slow-cooking method is a great way to get simmering flavors to blend together. This is a great example.

6 to 8 chicken breast halves
8 ozs. blue cheese salad dressing
1 (10 3/4-oz.) can fat-free cream of chicken or mushroom
  soup
1/2 cup water
1 (8-oz.) can sliced water chestnuts,
  drained
1 (2-oz.) jar pimentos, drained
1/4 cup chopped green onions, optional

15 MIN.

1. Place chicken breasts in slow cooker and add all other ingredients, except the green onions.
2. Set slow cooker on High for 1 hour and turn down to Low for another 7 hours.
3. Add green onions, if desired, during last 30 minutes of cooking time.
4. Serve with rice or pasta.

Serves 6 to 8.
Andy Roberts

GLEASON'S TIME-SAVER SPECIAL

These are often the best kind of recipes when there aren't enough hours in the day -- easy and good.

2 to 3 lbs. boneless, skinless chicken breasts
1/4 tsp. salt
1/2 tsp. black pepper
1 tbl. garlic powder
1 (10 3/4-oz.) can cream of mushroom soup
1 (10 3/4-oz.) can Cheddar cheese soup
1 (10-oz.) can Ro-tel tomatoes
1 (8-oz.) package egg noodles

1. Place chicken breasts into slow cooker and sprinkle with salt, pepper, and garlic powder.
2. Pour soups and tomatoes over all and cook on Low for 8 hours.
3. Add in package of noodles, pushing them down into the sauce to cover. Replace lid and cook for an additional 30 minutes on High.

Serves 4 to 6.
Jerri Gleason

You may also use pork instead of chicken for a change.

MINI-BOWL BITES

Looking for something to serve for a Super Bowl party or buffet? Help yourself!

1 to 2 lbs. boneless, skinless chicken thighs
1 large onion, chopped
1 red bell pepper, chopped
1 green bell pepper, chopped
1/4 cup chicken broth
Cracked black pepper to taste
1/2 cup barbecue sauce
1 cup shredded Monterey Jack cheese
Dinner rolls

15 MIN.

1. Place onion and bell peppers in slow cooker and top with chicken thighs.
2. Pour chicken broth over chicken. Season with cracked black pepper and cook on Low for 6 to 8 hours. At the end of cooking time, drain liquid from pot and shred chicken.
3. Return chicken to slow cooker and mix in barbecue sauce. Cook another 30 minutes.
4. Spoon mixture into split dinner rolls and top with shredded Monterey Jack cheese.

Serves 12 to15.

This is a favorite with children. Using small split rolls makes these sandwiches ideal for little hands.

SLOW-COOKED CHICKEN GRAVY

A family favorite was born out of time deprivation. After children are grown, it is one for the memory book.

1 whole fryer chicken
1 (1.25-oz.) packet golden onion soup mix or
   regular onion soup mix
1 (10 3/4-oz.) can cream of chicken soup
1/2 cup water
Black pepper to taste

1. Clean chicken and place in slow cooker.
2. In a medium-size bowl, mix remaining ingredients with a whisk until blended well.
3. Pour mixture over chicken; cover and cook on Low for 6 to 8 hours. Serve with rice.

Serves 4.
Tina Achord

Cornish hens or turkey breast may be substituted for chicken.

APRICOT CORNISH HENS

Two Cornish hens will fit easily in a 3 1/2- to 4-quart slow cooker. If you will be cooking four, the 5- to 6-quart oval cookers work nicely.

2 Cornish game hens
1/2 cup all-fruit apricot jam
1 (1-oz.) packet dried onion soup mix
1/3 cup Catalina salad dressing

10 MIN.

1. Place Cornish hens into slow cooker.
2. In a small bowl, mix apricot jam, onion soup mix, and Catalina salad dressing together and spoon over hens.
3. Cook on Low for 8 hours.

Serves 2 to 4.

This makes a great alternative to ham or turkey for a Thanksgiving or Easter dinner.

FRUITED CHICKEN

Sometimes, especially over the holidays, the fast lane is impossible to navigate. Try this stress-buster.

1 whole fryer chicken
1 (10-oz.) jar orange marmalade
2 oranges, cut and quartered, with skin on
Hot cooked rice or orzo

5 MIN.

1. Place fryer in slow cooker and top with orange marmalade, reserving a small amount for basting later.
2. Add quartered oranges and cook on Low for 6 to 8 hours.
3. Remove fryer from slow cooker, baste with reserved marmalade, and serve with rice or orzo.

Serves 4 to 6.

For a touch of fresh color, garnish with fresh orange slices. Orzo is a tiny pasta that resembles rice and may be used as a rice substitute.

LEMON-HERB CHICKEN

Some of the most popular slow-cooker recipes are those with only a few ingredients.

1 whole fryer chicken or 2 lbs. chicken pieces
4 cloves garlic, minced
1/2 cup butter or margarine, divided
1 (1.8-oz.) packet Knorr Classic Sauces,
  Lemon Herb Sauce Mix
3/4 cup water

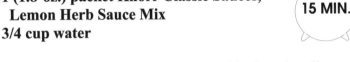

1. Place chicken in slow cooker. Add minced garlic.
2. Melt 1/4 cup butter or margarine in microwavable bowl. With wire whisk, stir in sauce mix until blended. Stir in 3/4 cup water and microwave on high power for 2 to 3 minutes until thickened. Stir twice.
3. Cut the other 1/4 cup butter or margarine into small pieces and place on top of chicken.
4. Pour sauce over all and cook on Low for 6 to 8 hours.

Serves 4.

Slice fresh lemons and parsley for a flavorful and colorful garnish. Serve with pasta or rice.

SEASONED TURKEY, MEACHAM-STYLE

Injecting poultry is a way to drive home flavors in the slow cooker.

3 lbs. split turkey breast or other pieces
Garlic juice, to taste
Poultry seasoning injector
1 tsp. garlic powder
1 tsp. onion powder
1 tsp. dried parsley
1 tsp. chili powder
Salt to taste, optional
1 tbl. cracked black pepper

15 MIN.

1. Inject turkey pieces with garlic juice. Place in slow cooker.
2. In a small bowl, mix seasonings together and sprinkle over poultry.
3. Cook on Low for 8 hours.

Serves 4 to 6.
Allyson Meacham

For seasoning beef, try dried onion soup mix, water, and red wine. To accompany pork, there's lemon pepper, garlic pepper, and salt.

PETITE HOLIDAY TURKEY

Preparing a turkey dinner can be daunting in smaller households of one or two people, especially when it comes to the holidays. Put the slow cooker to work for you and try a turkey breast.

1 (2 1/2-lb.) half turkey breast
2 small onions
4 to 6 new potatoes
3 carrots, sliced
2 cloves garlic, minced
1 cup sliced celery
1 bell pepper, sliced
1/2 cup white wine
3 tbls. all-purpose flour
2 tbls. crushed red pepper flakes

1. Place turkey breast in slow cooker and tuck onions, potatoes, and carrots along the sides. Add minced garlic, celery, and bell pepper.
2. In a small bowl, mix together wine and flour and pour over turkey. Sprinkle red pepper over all.
3. Cook on Low for 8 hours.

Serves 2 to 3.

 Feel free to add more seasonings. For those who prefer less "heat," leave out the red pepper and substitute salt and pepper to taste.

PICANTE CHICKEN

This recipe stems from a need to utilize picante sauce, which here in Louisiana seems to multiply in pantries. Picante sauce is a flavorful salsa that livens up just about any dish.

2 lbs. chicken pieces
1 tbl. blackened redfish seasoning
1 1/2 cups picante sauce
1 medium onion, quartered

10 MIN.

1. Place chicken in bottom of slow cooker. Sprinkle redfish seasoning liberally over chicken pieces.
2. Pour picante sauce over all and add onion. Cook on Low for 8 to 10 hours. You may also add more picante sauce in the last 15 minutes of cooking time, if desired.
3. Serve with noodles or rice.

Serves 4 to 6.
Tommy Simmons

CHICKEN AND BROCCOLI QUICHE

The slow cooker is a convenient way for caregivers to prepare a nutritious, easy meal for those who are ill.

2 tbls. canola oil
2 lbs. chicken breasts, boneless and skinless
1 (10-oz.) package frozen chopped broccoli, partially thawed
3/4 cup all-purpose flour
3/4 tsp. baking powder
1/2 tsp. salt, optional
1 cup evaporated milk
2 eggs, beaten
1 cup shredded low-fat Cheddar cheese
2 tbls. chopped onion
2 tsps. dried parsley flakes

PREP   TIME
15 MIN.

1. Coat slow cooker with canola oil. Place chicken and broccoli in cooker and cook on Low for 5 to 8 hours or on High for 3 to 4 hours, or until fork tender.
2. In separate bowl, stir together flour, baking powder, salt, evaporated milk, and eggs.
3. Fold in cheese, onion, and parsley. Pour mixture over chicken and cook 1 hour on High.

Serves 6.
Alicia Rourk

The moist heat of the slow cooker makes many foods soft and easier to chew for those who need it.Whenever possible, add onions, green peppers, and vegetables for an all-in-one-pot good nutrition factor.

SPANISH CHICKEN

Favorite recipes are often created to help busy families. A mother of two children under the age of five shared this tasty entrée.

3 to 4 boneless, skinless chicken breast halves, cut into large pieces
4 to 6 chicken thighs, bone in, remove skin
Salt, pepper, and paprika to taste
Garlic salt, optional
1 to 2 tsps. minced garlic
1 (6-oz.) can tomato paste
3/4 cup white wine
3/4 cup black olives, cut in half
3/4 cup large stuffed green olives, cut in half (retain liquid)

PREP TIME
15 MIN.

1. Season washed chicken with salt, pepper, paprika, and garlic salt and place in slow cooker.
2. In a small bowl, combine minced garlic, tomato paste, and wine and pour over chicken.
3. Add black and green olives to cooker, along with 4 to 6 tablespoons of the green olive vinegar.
4. Cover and cook on Low for 7 to 9 hours. (Separate chicken pieces once or twice during cooking.)
5. Serve over rice cooked in chicken broth, with paprika and dried parsley to taste.

Serves 4.
Wendy Magill

TARRAGON CHICKEN

Chicken recipes are often the most requested slow-cooker recipes. Dress up everyday chicken by trying some of the fresh herbs and variety of spices on grocery shelves and enjoy.

1 tbl. olive oil
1 whole fryer chicken
1 bunch green onions, chopped
1 (14 1/2-oz.) can chicken broth
1/4 cup white wine
1/4 cup butter, melted
1 clove garlic, minced
1 tbl. fresh chopped tarragon or 1 tsp. dried

PREP   TIME
10 MIN.

1. Grease stoneware insert of crockery cooker with olive oil.
2. Place whole chicken into slow cooker with chopped green onions.
3. Pour chicken broth over chicken along with white wine and butter.
4. Sprinkle minced garlic and tarragon over chicken. Cook on Low for 6 to 8 hours. Chicken will be falling-off-the-bone tender.

Serves 4 to 6.

SLOWER COOKERS KEEP RIGHT

If you have an herb garden, fresh herbs are delightful in flavoring slow-cooked dishes. Don't be afraid to experiment.

CHICKEN ENCHILADA

This is a good recipe for teens learning to cook. Let them add or subtract ingredients, substituting with ones they enjoy.

5 to 6 boneless, skinless chicken thighs
1 (1.25-oz.) package enchilada or taco seasoning mix
1 (6-oz.) can tomato paste
1/3 cup chicken broth
1 cup shredded hot pepper cheese
1/2 cup sour cream
1/4 cup sliced green onions
1/4 cup chopped green bell pepper
1 1/2 cups crushed tortilla chips

PREP   TIME

15 MIN.

1. Place boneless, skinless chicken thighs in slow cooker. In a small bowl, combine dry enchilada or taco mix with tomato paste and chicken broth to make a thick sauce.
2. Spread over chicken. Cover and cook on Low for 7 to 8 hours.
3. Turn cooker to High. Add cheese and stir until cheese melts. Remove to platter and top with sour cream.
4. Sprinkle with green onions and green pepper. Top with crushed tortilla chips.

Serves 6.

SLOW AND EASY TURKEY/CHICKEN

Cooking chicken or turkey in the slow cooker and freezing it for future chicken/turkey salad sandwiches is one way to prepare ahead for busy days.

8 to 10 turkey legs or chicken pieces
1 small onion, chopped
2 stalks celery, chopped
Salt and pepper to taste
1/2 cup water

PREP TIME

10 MIN.

1. Place turkey legs, onion, and celery in slow cooker.
2. Sprinkle salt and pepper over all and add water.
3. Cook on Low for 8 hours.
4. When turkey legs are cooked, debone and cool in refrigerator.
5. Freeze poultry in small freezer bags until ready to use.

Makes approximately 4 cups.

Freeze in proportion-sized bags for the amount needed for family-size casseroles, salads, and sandwiches.

HOT CHICKEN WINGS

Slow cookers are great for party buffets and get-togethers. Appetizers can remain warm at buffet tables for the length of the party.

**3 lbs. chicken wings, trimmed, or
   drummettes**
1 (12-oz.) bottle chili sauce
1/2 tsp. hot pepper sauce
1/2 tsp. garlic powder

1. Place wings in slow cooker and pour chili sauce over all.
2. Sprinkle hot sauce and garlic powder on wings before cooking on Low for 6 to 8 hours.
3. Serve with extra chili sauce if desired.

Serves 12.

MUSHROOM CHICKEN

Chicken is a favorite in the slow cooker.

1 1/2 cups brown rice
1 medium onion, chopped
1 tsp. salt
1 tsp. pepper
1 (10 3/4-oz.) can reduced-fat cream of mushroom soup
2 (7-oz.) cans mushroom pieces, with liquid
4 chicken breast halves or thighs
1/2 cup water

PREP TIME

15 MIN.

1. Spray stoneware insert with non-stick cooking spray. Pour in rice and add chopped onion, salt, and pepper.
2. In medium-size bowl, mix cream of mushroom soup with mushrooms and liquid from both cans of mushrooms. Pour half of mixture over rice.
3. Place chicken pieces on top of rice and sauce and pour remaining sauce mixture over chicken.
4. Add 1/2 cup of water and cook on Low for 8 hours.

Serves 4.

Chicken pieces may be skinned just before eating or cooking. Buy skinless chicken for an added convenience factor. It makes no difference to the recipe itself. The liquid from the canned mushrooms can be valuable in this recipe. Remember not to drain mushrooms before placing in cooker.

DRUNK CHICKEN

This is one of our family recipes which has been adapted to the slow cooker. Don't be afraid to adapt your own specialties. Most will slow cook very well.

8 chicken pieces
1 (10 3/4-oz.) can cream of celery soup
1 (8-oz.) package fresh mushrooms
Cracked black pepper
1/4 cup sherry

PREP TIME
10 MIN.

1. Place chicken pieces in slow cooker.
2. Top with soup, mushrooms, cracked pepper, and sherry.
3. Cook on Low for 8 hours and serve with rice.

Serves 6.

For a little lagniappe, which means "something extra" here in the Bayou, melt 1/4 cup butter or margarine and mix with Parmesan cheese to taste. Pour over rice.

CHICKEN TACOS

If you know the following day will be especially hectic, plan ahead, and dinner will be ready when you get home from that last errand, work, or picking up the children.

12 chicken tenders, cut into bite-size pieces
1/2 cup taco sauce
1 (1.25-oz.) package taco seasoning mix
1 (2-oz.) can chopped green chilies
Shredded Cheddar cheese
Sour cream
Flour tortillas

10 MIN.

1. Place chicken into slow cooker and top with taco sauce.
2. Pour taco seasoning over all and add green chilies. Cook on Low for 8 hours.
3. Remove from slow cooker and spoon into each tortilla, topping with Cheddar cheese and sour cream.

Serves 6 to 8.

If your children dislike spicy foods, leave out the green chilies and top with a little extra taco sauce.

STUFFED CHICKEN

Retirees, caretakers and even teens enjoy the simplicity of slow cooking. This recipe is an adaptation of a family favorite.

1 (6-oz.) canister Stove-Top stuffing mix, any flavor
1/4 cup white wine
1 (16-oz.) bag fresh baby carrots
6 boneless, skinless chicken breast halves
1 onion, cut into quarters
Cracked black pepper, to taste

PREP TIME 15 MIN.

1. Prepare stuffing according to package directions.
2. Add white wine and stir.
3. Place baby carrots and onions in slow cooker and top with 3 chicken breasts. For the next layer, add half of stuffing, then place remaining chicken breasts on top of stuffing.
4. Sprinkle with cracked black pepper and top with remaining stuffing.
5. Cover and cook on Low for 8 hours.

Serves 4 to 6.

You may substitute your own special stuffing recipe if you prefer; however, the convenience mix does save time.

CHILI-TOPPED CHICKEN

This is a meal you'll be happy to come home to.

4 to 6 boneless, skinless chicken breast halves
1/2 cup all-purpose flour
2 tbls. black pepper
3 tbls. vegetable oil
1/2 cup chili sauce
1/4 cup steak sauce

1. Mix flour and pepper together in plastic container and dredge chicken breasts in mixture, coating well.
2. In a skillet, brown chicken breasts in oil over medium-high heat and place chicken into slow cooker.
3. Mix together chili sauce and steak sauce and pour over chicken. Cook on Low for 6 to 8 hours.

Serves 4 to 6.

You can add additional chili sauce toward the end of cooking time for a more intense flavor and brighter color. Garnish with a few sprigs of fresh parsley for added color.

BLACK BEAN AND CHICKEN WRAP

These wraps are nice for an informal luncheon or a light dinner.

1 lb. chicken tenders
1 (4-oz.) can diced green chilies
1 (16-oz.) can black beans, undrained
1 (14 1/2-oz.) can diced tomatoes, drained
3 green onions, chopped
1 1/2 cups shredded Cheddar cheese
1/2 cup sour cream
6 to 8 flour tortillas

PREP TIME

10 MIN.

1. Place chicken tenders, chilies, beans, and tomatoes into slow cooker. Cook on Low for 6 to 8 hours.
2. Remove from slow cooker with slotted spoon and place in tortillas with green onions, cheese, and a small dollop of sour cream. Roll up and secure with toothpick until ready to eat. Top with extra cheese if desired.

Serves 6.

TEMPLE'S BRISKET

The slow cooker can't be beat when it comes to tenderizing a good brisket. Use a 5- to 6-quart cooker for this.

1 (5- to 7-lb.) beef brisket
1 bulb garlic, divided into cloves
6 tbls. Tony Chachere's Original Seasoning
2 tsps. red pepper
1 onion, chopped
2 (10 3/4-oz.) cans cream of mushroom soup
1/2 cup water
Cornstarch, for thickening
1/4 cup water
2 tbls. Kitchen Bouquet (more if needed)

PREP TIME 15 MIN.

1. Trim brisket of fat. Peel and cut each garlic clove in half. Stud meat with garlic pieces. Generously sprinkle Tony Chachere's and red pepper over meat.
2. Add onion, soups, and 1/2 cup water. (You may use the reduced-fat mushroom soups if desired).
3. Cook on Low for 8 to10 hours. Remove brisket and allow liquid in slow cooker to cool. As fat rises to the top, skim off and discard. Mix 4 tablespoons cornstarch in 1/4 cup water and add to liquid in cooker for thickening of gravy. Add Kitchen Bouquet for color.
4. Slice brisket and serve.

Serves 8.
Wayne Temple

SLOWER COOKERS KEEP RIGHT Beef briskets can be found already trimmed of the fat, or you can buy them at a slightly lower price and trim them yourself. (See recipe for "Second Time Around" on Page 41).

BRISKET, SECOND TIME AROUND

Shredded brisket
3/4 cup barbecue sauce
3 tbls. brown sugar
1 tsp. lemon juice
1/4 cup Steen's cane syrup
Cayenne pepper to taste
2 tbls. Worcestershire sauce
Scant amount water

1. Preheat oven to 300 degrees. Mix all the liquid ingredients and seasonings together.
2. Place shredded beef in heavy-duty foil packets on a cookie sheet. Top with enough sauce to coat beef.
3. Bake in a 300-degree oven for 1 to 1 1/2 hours.
4. Remove packets from oven. Open carefully and spoon beef onto buns.

Serves 4 to 6.
Wayne Temple

 This is a great kid-friendly recipe.

FRONTIER BEAN CASSEROLE

Rather than simple pork and beans, this is a mixture of several different varieties of beans, creating a unique flavor.

1 lb. lean ground beef or ground chuck
1 medium onion, chopped
1 tsp. salt
1/2 tsp. black pepper
1/2 tsp. chili powder
1 tbl. prepared mustard
1/4 cup ketchup
1/4 cup barbecue sauce
1/4 cup brown sugar
1/4 cup granulated sugar
1 (16-oz.) can pork and beans, drained
1 (14 3/4-oz.) can lima beans, drained
1 (15 1/2-oz.) can red kidney beans, drained

PREP TIME 15 MIN.

1. Cook meat in skillet over medium-high heat. Drain; add onion, salt, pepper, and chili powder, mixing well.
2. Place in slow cooker and add all other ingredients. Stir and cook on Low for 6 to 8 hours.

Serves 6 to 8.

Recipe can be doubled; just watch the size of your cooker. Use a 5- to 6-quart cooker if you are doubling recipe.

BEEF FAJITAS

Children enjoy having choices, so experiment with the toppings and give them lots to choose from, including different varieties of cheeses and salsas.

1 1/2 lbs. beef flank steak
1 cup onion, chopped
1 green bell pepper, cut into strips
1/8 cup jalapeño pepper, chopped, optional
1 tbl. chopped parsley
1/4 tsp. garlic powder
1 tbl. Worcestershire sauce
1 tsp. chili powder
1/2 tsp. salt, optional
1 (14.5-oz.) can chopped tomatoes
12 (8-inch) flour tortillas
Toppings: sour cream, guacamole, shredded
  cheese, and salsa

PREP TIME
15 MIN.

1. Cut flank steak into six pieces. Combine meat, onion, bell pepper, jalapeño, parsley, garlic powder, Worcestershire sauce, chili powder, and salt. Stir mixture and add tomatoes.
2. Cover and cook on Low for 8 to10 hours or on High for 4 to 5 hours. Remove meat from slow cooker and shred.
3. Return meat to slow cooker and stir. To serve fajitas, spread meat mixture in center of flour tortillas.
4. Top with sour cream, guacamole, shredded cheese, and salsa as optional toppings. Roll up tortillas and serve.

Serves 6 to 8.
Alicia Rourk

CHUCK STEAK IN BEER

Some recipes call for a few more ingredients than slow-cooker enthusiasts like to see, but many are worth it. This is one that is.

1 tbl. butter or margarine
1 tbl. canola oil
1 (2-lb.) boneless beef chuck shoulder steak, cut 1 1/2 inches
  thick
Salt and pepper
1 onion, sliced in rings
1 tsp. crushed red pepper flakes, divided
1/2 cup beer
3/4 cup onion-flavored beef broth
1/2 cup chopped parsley
2 cloves garlic, minced
6 sprigs fresh thyme or 1/2 tsp. dried thyme leaves
2 bay leaves
1 large baking potato, peeled and thinly sliced

PREP TIME 15 MIN.

1. Heat butter and oil in Dutch oven over medium heat until hot. Add beef steak. Brown 5 to 6 minutes, turning once. Season with salt and pepper, as desired. Remove steak and place in slow cooker.
2. In same Dutch oven, add onion and cook for 4 to 5 minutes or until soft, stirring often. Stir in 1/2 tsp. crushed red pepper flakes.
3. Place mixture in slow cooker. Pour beer and broth over steak; add parsley, garlic, thyme, and bay leaves.
4. Place potato slices over steak and sprinkle with remaining red pepper flakes. Cook on Low for 8 hours.

Serves 4.

 REDUCE SPEED For a time-saver, peel and slice potato the night before and place in cold water in the refrigerator.

CORBIN'S TOMATO STEAK

This is one of those "Open the pantry and see what you can put together" types of recipes. It is basic home cooking at its best.

2 lbs. round steak, cut into serving size pieces
1 (10 3/4-oz.) can tomato soup
1 bunch green onions, chopped
2 stalks celery, chopped
1 tbl. cayenne pepper
1 clove garlic, minced
1/2 cup water
1/4 cup all-purpose flour

10 MIN.

1. Place round steak into slow cooker and sprinkle with cayenne pepper.
2. Add all other ingredients, except flour.
3. Cook on Low for 6 to 8 hours. Stir in flour during last 30 minutes of cooking time.
4. Serve over pasta shells or rice.

Seves 4 to 6.
Alma Corbin

It isn't necessary to brown the round steak; however, some prefer the seared flavor.

CREOLE POT ROAST

Chuck roast is one of my favorite comfort foods in the slow cooker. This Louisiana-style roast is filled with Creole flavor.

1 (2- to 3-lb.) boneless chuck roast, browned
3 tbls. vegetable oil
1 (16-oz.) package baby carrots, or 3 to 4 whole, peeled and
  sliced
3 medium potatoes, peeled and cut in half
3 medium onions, peeled and quartered
1 (15-oz.) can tomato sauce
3/4 cup Spanish olives
1/4 cup olive juice
3 tsps. Tabasco sauce
1 tsp. Worcestershire sauce

1. In Dutch oven, brown roast in oil.
2. Place vegetables at bottom of the stoneware insert. Place roast on top and cover with remaining ingredients.
3. Cook on Low for 6 to 8 hours.

Serves 4 to 6.
Linda Holloway

BEEF TORTILLAS

When another school year gets under way, try a kid-friendly recipe. What could be more welcome than a beef tortilla?

1 lb. ground beef
1 (10 3/4-oz.) can Italian tomato soup
1/8 tsp. basil
1 cup thick and chunky salsa
1/4 cup milk
6 flour tortillas or 8 corn tortillas, cut into 1-inch strips
1 cup shredded Cheddar cheese

PREP TIME

15 MIN.

1. Brown ground beef in skillet over medium-high heat.
2. Place beef in slow cooker. Mix soup, basil, and salsa and pour over ground beef. Cook on Low for 6 to 8 hours.
3. During last hour of cooking time, add milk and stir. Add tortilla strips, forming a lattice design.
4. Sprinkle cheese over all just before serving.

Serves 4 to 6.

HASH-BROWN WINNER

Casseroles are great in the slow cooker. This one has the added convenience factor of using frozen hash browns. It's a definite winner on the time-saver scale. Give the children a chance to help with this one.

6 frozen hash-brown patties, slightly thawed
1 lb. ground chuck
1 medium onion, chopped
1 (10-oz.) can diced tomatoes and chilies
1 (10 3/4-oz.) can cream of celery soup
1 1/2 cups shredded Cheddar cheese

PREP TIME
15 MIN.

1. Position 4 hash-brown patties in bottom and along sides, if needed, of slow cooker.
2. In a skillet, brown ground chuck and onion over medium-high heat; drain and put mixture on top of hash browns.
3. Mix together diced tomatoes and chilies with cream of celery soup and pour over beef mixture in slow cooker.
4. Top with 2 hash-brown patties and 1/2 cup Cheddar cheese. Cook on Low for 6 to 8 hours. During last half hour of cooking, add remaining Cheddar cheese.

Serves 4 to 6.

SCHOOL ZONE — Most youngsters enjoy hash browns and hamburger mixtures of any kind. Cheese is also generally popular. Supervise while they pour and measure, and they will become assistant chefs in no time.

GARLIC HERB STEAK

*Want to encourage your family to eat vegetables? Try this dish.
Shredding makes them hardly noticeable.*

**1 (3- to 4-lb.) round steak, cut into 4 sections suitable for
rolling**
1 cup shredded carrots
1/2 cup chopped onions
1/4 cup chopped celery
1 medium yellow squash, shredded
1 (15-oz.) can garlic herb tomato sauce

PREP TIME

15 MIN.

1. Cut round steak into four sections. In a medium-size bowl,
   combine carrots, onions, celery, and squash and place
   approximately four tablespoons of vegetable mixture in the
   center of each piece of steak. Roll and tie each filled piece of
   steak with kitchen string.
2. Place into slow cooker and pour half of sauce on steaks. Add
   in any leftover vegetable mixture.
3. Set slow cooker on Low and cook for 8 hours. During the last
   45 minutes of cooking time, pour off accumulated liquid
   carefully and add remaining sauce.
4. Remove from slow cooker.

Serves 4.

Near the end of cooking time, drain any accumulated
liquid (there should only be a little) and top with
remaining sauce. Before serving, remove ties. You
may use toothpicks to hold rolls together when you
place on a serving platter, but remember to remove them
before eating!

Because of the lengthy cooking time and accumulating liquid,
don't be afraid to add spices when you're slow cooking.

JALAPEÑO ROUND STEAK

Slow cooking doesn't have to mean tasteless. A well-chosen selection of seasonings is the heart of many Louisiana recipes.

3 to 4 lbs. round steak, cut into cubes
3 tbls. olive oil
1 tbl. Tony Chachere's Original Seasoning
2 cloves garlic, minced
1 bunch green onions, chopped
1 green bell pepper, chopped
1 jalapeño pepper, chopped
1/4 cup chopped celery
8 ozs. fresh chopped mushrooms
Tabasco sauce to taste
2 tsps. soy sauce
1 (0.75-oz.) package Cajun brown gravy mix
1 cup water

PREP TIME
15 MIN.

1. In a large skillet, brown round steak over medium-high heat in olive oil. Sprinkle with Tony Chachere's seasoning. Place in slow cooker.
2. Add garlic, onions, bell pepper, jalapeño pepper, celery, and mushrooms. Sprinkle with Tabasco and soy sauce and sprinkle packet of gravy mix over all. Add water.
3. Cook on Low for 8 hours. Serve over rice.

Serves 4 to 6.

If you cannot find Cajun gravy mix in your area, increase the amount of Tabasco and use regular brown gravy mix.

PACKED POTATOES

This is one of those time-saver favorites sure to be popular with most family members, even the pickiest.

1 lb. ground sirloin
1 onion, chopped
1 (15-oz.) can Mexicorn
1 (10-oz.) can Ro-tel tomatoes
1 (16-oz.) can red kidney beans
1 (1 1/4-oz.) package enchilada sauce mix
1/4 cup water
4 baking potatoes

1. In a skillet, sauté onion over medium heat and add ground sirloin. Brown and place mixture in slow cooker.
2. Add Mexicorn, Ro-tel tomatoes, kidney beans, enchilada sauce mix, and 1/4 cup water.
3. Cook on Low for 6 to 8 hours.
4. Bake potatoes and split in half when done. Using a slotted spoon, fill potatoes with slow-cooked mixture and top with toppings of choice, such as grated cheese, sour cream, chopped green onions, or jalapeño pepper slices for a spicier flavor.

Serves 4.

LIMA BEAN PIE

Some of the older recipes are the ones that bring back good memories. Converting them to slow cooking isn't hard, and a comfort food is reborn.

1 lb. ground beef
1 onion, chopped
2 (15.5-oz.) cans lima beans
1 green bell pepper, chopped
1 (27.75-oz.) jar prepared spaghetti sauce
1 (6-oz.) package Mexican cornbread mix
1 cup shredded Cheddar cheese

PREP   TIME
15 MIN.

1. In a skillet, cook ground beef with onion over medium heat. Place beef and onion in slow cooker and add lima beans, bell pepper, and spaghetti sauce.
2. Mix Mexican cornbread mix as directed on package and spread batter over mixture in slow cooker.
3. Cook on High for 1 hour and turn to Low for 4 to 5 hours. Sprinkle Cheddar cheese over all and serve.

Serves 4 to 6.

 When converting old favorites to slow-cooker recipes, watch the liquid content; you may need to cut back. Also, you may need to increase the amount of seasonings.

TOP-OF-THE-DAY MARINATED BEEF

Tougher and usually less expensive cuts of beef do very well in the slow-cooking process. Take advantage of them. A spinach salad and a fresh loaf of French bread go well with this dish.

4 lbs. top round steak, cut into strips
1/3 cup olive oil
1 1/2 cups red wine
1 tsp. dried basil leaves
1 tsp. dried ground thyme
1 tbl. cracked black pepper
6 slices bacon
2 onions, sliced
3 cloves garlic, minced
1 lb. fresh mushrooms, sliced
1/2 cup all-purpose flour

PREP TIME
15 MIN.

1. Mix steak marinade of olive oil, red wine, basil, thyme, and black pepper in plastic container large enough to accommodate meat. Add steak strips and marinate overnight in the refrigerator.
2. In a skillet, fry bacon. Turn heat down to medium-low and add in onions, garlic, and mushrooms, sautéing until vegetables are limp.
3. Place beef in slow cooker, reserving marinade. Pour flour over meat, mixing to coat. Add bacon-mushroom mixture to slow cooker and pour marinade over all ingredients.
4. Cook on Low for 8 hours. Serve over broad egg noodles.

Serves 4 to 6.

 This recipe requires extra time for morning preparations since you'll be frying bacon and sautéing onion, garlic, and mushrooms.

MEATBALL SUBS

This is one of those easy lunch or dinner specials sure to please most family members. Add potato salad and cole slaw to round out the meal.

4 to 5 frozen meatballs per sub sandwich (16 to 20 meatballs for 4 subs)
1 (26 3/4-oz.) can prepared spaghetti sauce
1 (8-oz.) package shredded mozzarella cheese
Sub rolls

10 MIN.

1. Place thawed meatballs in slow cooker and pour spaghetti sauce over all.
2. Cook on High for 4 hours.
3. When cooked, remove meatballs with slotted spoon and place in subs.
4. Spoon sauce over meatballs and top with cheese.

Serves 4.

Children of all ages love this recipe. Frozen meatballs add to the convenience factor, but you may use your own homemade meatballs, if desired.

VALERIE'S MEXICAN MIX

If you're looking for a change of pace for lunch, Valerie's Mexican Mix, along with potato salad, cole slaw, or chips just might fit the bill. If you're even more adventuresome and have restless children at home, grab a blanket, find a shady tree, and have a picnic on your lawn.

2 lbs. stew meat, diced
1 (1.25-oz.) package taco seasoning mix
1/3 cup water
Taco shells or pita pockets

1. Place stew meat, cut into small pieces, in the slow cooker.
2. Pour taco seasoning mix over meat and add water.
3. Cook on Low for 6 to 8 hours.
4. Spoon into taco shells or pita pockets.

Serves 4 to 6.
Valerie Bauer

You may use hard or soft taco shells and add shredded lettuce and cheese, if you like.

BASIC HOMESTYLE ROAST

When I'm asked for a good beginning recipe, I usually recommend either a simple chicken recipe or a basic roast. They're good comfort foods and great family fare.

3 potatoes, halved
3 carrots, sliced lengthwise
2 small onions, halved
1 (3-lb.) boneless chuck roast
Cracked black pepper, to taste
1 (1-oz.) packet dried onion soup mix
1/2 cup water

PREP TIME
10 MIN.

1. Place potatoes, carrots, and onions in bottom of slow cooker. Add roast, cutting in half or thirds to fit size of cooker.
2. Sprinkle black pepper over roast as desired. Pour contents of onion soup mix packet over all. Add water.
3. Cook on Low for 8 to 10 hours. Remove roast and vegetables to serving platter. Liquid may be used as a light gravy.

Serves 8.

STOP Be careful not to add too much liquid. Slow cooking creates its own moisture. Place all sliced carrots, onions, and halved potatoes in the bottom of the cooker, forming a "rack" for the meat. The vegetables need the direct source of heat. Slow-cooking experts caution that the appliance shouldn't be more than two-thirds full.

ROULADEN

Be sure to use a 5- to 6-quart slow cooker for this one.

10 (1/4-inch) thick slices bottom round steak
1/2 lb. sliced, uncooked bacon
1 large onion, chopped
1/4 cup prepared mustard
Salt and pepper (white or black), to taste
Peppercorns, as desired
1 bay leaf
1 (1-oz.) packet dried onion soup mix
2 tbls. margarine, melted
1 tsp. prepared mustard
1/4 cup all-purpose flour

1. To make filling, mix uncooked bacon with onion, mustard, salt, and white or black pepper. Set aside.
2. Trim fatty tissue off steak. Pound with meat hammer just enough to tenderize; divide filling equally onto each steak slice. Flatten mounded filling and roll up beef in jelly-roll fashion, starting with the more tapered end.
3. Secure steak rolls with toothpicks or string. Brown on all sides in skillet over medium-high heat.
4. Place in a 5- or 6-quart slow cooker, scraping up any remnants in pan and placing on top of Rouladen. Add peppercorns, bay leaf, and onion soup mix. Cook on Low for 6 to 8 hours.
5. At end of cooking time, remove beef rolls. Place 2 tablespoons melted margarine and a teaspoon of mustard into liquid in the slow cooker. In a separate small container, mix 1/4 cup of flour with enough liquid taken from slow cooker to make a paste, and stir into margarine/gravy mixture.

Serves 6 to 8.
Eleonor Rice

SPAGHETTI ROAST

Here's a time-saver recipe for the most hectic of days. It also should make enough for leftovers.

1 (3-lb.) chuck roast
2 tbls. vegetable oil
3 cups prepared spaghetti sauce
1/2 tsp. ground oregano
2 medium onions, quartered
4 cloves garlic, minced
1 (8-oz.) package fresh mushrooms, sliced
1 lb. angel hair pasta

PREP TIME
10 MIN.

1. In a Dutch oven, brown chuck roast over medium-high heat in oil.
2. Place roast in slow cooker and add all other ingredients, except pasta.
3. Cook on Low for 8 hours.
4. Slice and serve over bed of angel hair pasta.

Serves 6 to 8.

Use some of the leftover beef for a homemade vegetable soup.

STEAK PIZZIOLA

While we think of rib-eyes as a grilled treat, steaks can also make wonderful slow-cooker fare. Use a 5- to 6-quart slow cooker.

4 rib-eye steaks
1 (6-oz.) can tomato paste
1 (8-oz.) can tomato sauce
1 (28-oz.) jar Ragu spaghetti sauce, original flavor
1 green bell pepper, cut into strips
1 large onion, cut in strips
1 (8-oz.) package fresh mushrooms
1 (8-oz.) package grated mozzarella cheese
Parmesan cheese, to taste
Whole black olives

15 MIN.

1. Mix tomato paste, tomato sauce, and Ragu in a large bowl.
2. Place the first steak in slow cooker for bottom layer and spoon in just enough sauce to cover the meat.
3. Add a portion of the bell pepper, onions, mushrooms, cheeses, and whole black olives.
4. Layer again with second steak, sauce, cheeses, and vegetables. Do the same with third and fourth steak, layering as you go along until all steak, sauce, and vegetables are used.
5. Cover with remaining mozzarella and Parmesan cheeses. Cook on Low for 8 hours and garnish with remaining whole black olives.

Serves 4 to 6.
Betty Gayle Markins

SPEED
SLOW

Serve over pasta. Angel hair pasta works nicely. You can thicken sauce with Italian bread crumbs if desired.

STEAK ON THE RUN

A hearty meal for families on the go.

2 (1-lb.) boneless sirloin steaks, sliced thick
1/4 cup butter or margarine
8 ozs. fresh mushrooms, sliced
1 bunch green onion tops, sliced
1 (1-oz.) packet dried onion soup mix
1/3 cup sherry
1/4 cup water

15 MIN.

1. In a large skillet, brown steak slices over medium-high heat in butter or margarine.
2. Place browned meat into slow cooker. Add mushrooms, onions, dried onion soup, sherry, and water.
3. Set slow cooker on Low and cook for 8 hours. Serve over hot, buttered noodles.

Serves 4 to 6.

Browning the steak first in a small amount of margarine means a few extra minutes for preparation, but it often enhances the flavor.

TACO SALAD

Tacos in the slow cooker? Sure. It couldn't be easier with today's convenience taco salad shells, seasoning packets, and sauces.

1 1/2 lbs. lean ground beef
1 medium onion, chopped
1/4 cup chopped green bell pepper
1 (1.25-oz.) taco seasoning packet
1 (16-oz.) can red kidney beans
1/2 tsp. garlic powder
1/2 tsp. chili powder
1 (8-oz.) can tomato sauce
4 taco salad shells
1 cup shredded Mexican cheese
1 (8-oz.) jar taco sauce
Lettuce
Guacamole, optional

15 MIN.

1. In a skillet, brown ground beef over medium-high heat. Add in onions and cook until transparent.
2. Transfer beef and onions to slow cooker and add bell pepper, taco seasoning packet, kidney beans, and garlic and chili powders. Pour tomato sauce over all. Stir.
3. Cook on Low for 6 to 8 hours and, using a slotted spoon, place into taco salad shells lined with lettuce.
4. Top with Mexican cheese and taco sauce. Top with guacamole, if desired.

Serves 4.

Let children "build" their own taco salad to encourage their participation in food choices.

PIZZA HATS

*Here's a recipe that children of all ages appreciate. Try Pizza
Hats for a special luncheon or teen party.*

1/2 lb. ground beef
1/2 lb. ground sausage
1/8 tsp. dried, ground oregano
1/4 tsp. garlic powder
1 (14-oz.) jar pizza sauce
4 pita pocket breads
1/4 cup chopped green onion
1/2 cup chopped bell pepper
2 ozs. sliced pepperoni
Shredded mozzarella cheese
Parmesan cheese

1. In a skillet, brown ground beef and sausage over medium-
   high heat with oregano and garlic powder. Drain and place on
   a paper towel-lined plate to remove excess liquid.
2. Place beef and sausage in slow cooker and add pizza sauce.
3. Cook on Low for 3 hours.
4. Cut a circle out of top layer of pita bread, leaving at least a
   1-inch margin all the way around. Save circle cut-out.
5. Preheat oven to 400 degrees and place bottom of pita on
   cookie sheet and bake for 5 to 8 minutes.
6. Remove pitas from oven and cool. Divide slow-cooker
   mixture among pita bread circles and top with green onions,
   bell pepper, and pepperoni. Sprinkle with mozzarella cheese
   and top with reserved pita bread circle. Top with Parmesan
   cheese and return hat to oven for 7 minutes.

Serves 4.

 Children enjoy not only eating the hats, but creating them.

PINEAPPLE BEAN BAKE

If you are looking for a dish to take to the home of a friend who has been ill, had a new baby, or needs a little cheering up, this is a tasty and easy choice.

1 lb. ground beef
1 tbl. onion powder
1 (28-oz.) can pork and beans
1 (8-oz.) can pineapple chunks, drained
1 onion, chopped
1 bell pepper, chopped
2 tbls. Worcestershire sauce
2 garlic cloves, minced
1/2 tsp. black pepper
3/4 cup barbecue sauce

PREP TIME 15 MIN.

1. In a skillet, brown beef, sprinkled with onion powder, over medium-high heat and drain. Transfer to a 3 1/2- to 4-quart slow cooker; add remaining ingredients and mix well.
2. Cover and cook on Low for 4 to 6 hours.

Serves 6.

If you will be transporting slow-cooked meals, look for one of the insulated carriers available now for all sizes of slow cookers. Velcro straps secure the cooker, and the insulation keeps the dish warm. Handles make carrying easy.

ITALIAN BEEF SIRLOIN

If you read cooking magazines the way I do, let your imagination take flight as you read. Even sitting in a carpool line can be productive. Before you know it, ingredients change, spices get spicier, and ideas are born.

2 lbs. beef sirloin, sliced into thin strips
6 garlic cloves, peeled and diced
1 sprig fresh or 1 tbl. dried rosemary
3 tbls. olive oil, divided
1/2 cup light red wine
Cracked black pepper

PREP TIME
15 MIN.

1. The night before, combine beef, garlic, rosemary, and 1 tablespoon olive oil. Marinate in a covered container in the refrigerator overnight.
2. Heat remaining 2 tablespoons of olive oil in a skillet over medium-high heat and brown drained sirloin strips.
3. Place sirloin in slow cooker and add wine and cracked black pepper. Cook on Low for 8 hours and serve over broad egg noodles.

Serves 4.

 SPEED SLOW The alcohol content in the wine will cook out, leaving the resulting flavor in the beef. Between the marinating and slow cooking, the flavor permeates well. Enjoy.

ITALIAN BEEF BRISKET

Whether one is celebrating Mardi Gras or another special occasion, it's nice to have a "party" food. Laissez les bon temps rouler (Let the good times roll) and enjoy the food along the way.

1 (4- to 6-lb.) beef brisket
2 tbls. dried basil
1 tbl. crushed red pepper flakes
1 tbl. dried, ground oregano
1 (1-oz.) packet dried onion soup mix
4 cloves garlic
1 large onion, sliced
1 cup water

PREP TIME
15 MIN.

1. Mix basil, red pepper, oregano, and dried onion soup mix together.
2. Make four slits in brisket and place 1 garlic clove in each slit.
3. Rub spice and seasoning mixture into beef and place in slow cooker. Add water and place onion slices on top of beef.
4. Cook on Low for 8 hours. Remove from pot and shred beef, placing shredded beef back into the cooker for another 45 minutes.
5. Serve in hot crusty rolls.

Serves 12 to 15.
Kay Van Law

Be sure to rub the spice mixture into the beef well. Check that your spices are fresh. Old spices lose their zest.

BARBECUE BEEF BRISKET

This has been one of my most requested recipes and a favorite for any brisket fan. Use a 5- to 6-quart slow cooker.

1 (7- to 8-lb.) trimmed brisket
3 tsps. garlic powder
3 tsps. onion salt
2 tsps. celery salt
3 tsps. black pepper
2 tsps. meat tenderizer
3 tsps. Worcestershire sauce

PREP TIME
15 MIN.

1. Mix seasonings and rub on brisket, then place meat in covered container. Marinate in refrigerator overnight for 8 to 12 hours.
2. Place in a 5- to 6-quart slow cooker and cook on High for 4 hours.
3. Turn to Low and cook for another 8 hours, then remove brisket from cooker.
4. Drain, shred beef, then set meat aside.

Mix the following together:

3/4 cup ketchup
1/4 cup brown sugar
1 cup hickory-smoked barbecue sauce
1/2 cup beer

1. Place shredded beef back into slow cooker with above sauce and cook on Low for about 2 hours. Serve in sub rolls.

Serves 15.
Lynn Roberts

SPANISH-STYLE LIVER

If you are not a fan of liver, substitute round steak for this one and enjoy. Jalapeño tomatoes add the extra "zest."

2 lbs. sliced beef or calves liver
4 slices bacon, cut in half
1/2 cup chopped carrots
1/2 cup chopped celery
1 onion, sliced
1 (14 1/2-oz.) can jalapeño diced tomatoes, undrained
1/2 tsp. pepper
1 small bay leaf

PREP TIME

10 MIN.

1. Place liver in slow cooker and arrange bacon on top. Mix remaining ingredients and pour over liver.
2. Cover and cook on Low for 6 to 8 hours. Remove bay leaf and serve.

Serves 6.

SPEED SLOW

Liver should be nice and tender at the end of the slow-cooking process. If you like, top with crumbled cooked bacon for garnish.

FAST-TRACK NACHOS

Nachos are ever-popular with teenagers. Try this recipe, and you're sure to have a popular house for them to gather.

1 lb. lean ground beef
1 (4-oz.) can diced green chilies
2 cups chunky salsa
1 (16-oz.) can pinto beans, drained
1 (6-oz.) bag nacho chips
1 (8-oz.) package shredded mozzarella and Cheddar cheese
  blend

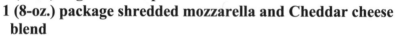

PREP TIME
15 MIN.

1. In a small skillet, cook ground beef and drain off grease. Put beef into slow cooker and add green chilies, salsa, and beans. Cook on Low for 6 hours.
2. If used as a main course, pour chips into casserole dish, crumble if desired, and top with beef mixture. Sprinkle cheese blend over all. For appetizers, use chips to dip into beef mixture.

Serves 6 to 8.

SCHOOL ZONE

By adding a green salad, you have an easy family dinner. If serving as a main course, the serving size is 4.

SAUSAGE AND BEEF MUFFINS

This is a great appetizer for a small gathering. The slow cooker keeps the mixture warm for the length of the party.

1/2 lb. lean ground beef
1 (16-oz.) package bulk hot sausage
1 (6-oz.) roll garlic cheese
English muffins

15 MIN.

1. In a skillet, brown ground beef and sausage. Drain and place in slow cooker.
2. Cut rolled cheese into sections and add to mixture in cooker. Cook on Low for 4 hours, stirring once after 2 hours.
3. Spoon onto toasted English muffins and serve.

Serves 6 to 8.

Recipe can easily be doubled for a larger gathering. If you prefer, serve with party crackers instead of muffins.

FLANK STEAK

Marinating works well for slow-cooker recipes by enhancing the flavor of the beef. The all-day cooking process then seals it in.

1 (3-lb.) flank steak, cut into 1-inch thick strips
1/4 cup soy sauce
1/4 cup brown sugar
3 tbls. Worcestershire sauce
1 tsp. garlic powder
1 bell pepper, sliced, optional

PREP TIME
10 MIN.

1. In a large bowl, mix soy sauce, brown sugar, Worcestershire sauce, and garlic powder. Prick flank steak strips with fork and place in mixture. Marinate steak in refrigerator overnight.
2. Place steak and marinade in slow cooker and cook on Low for 8 hours. Serve with rice and garnish with strips of bell pepper, if desired.

Serves 4.

PORK AND CRANBERRY ROAST

Pork and cranberry -- it's a combination hard to beat, especially when it's slow-cooked style. Use a 5- to 6-quart slow cooker.

1 (4- to 5-lb.) boneless pork roast
1 (12-oz.) bag whole cranberries
1 cup cranberry juice
2 medium onions, cut into quarters
1 (1-oz.) packet dried onion soup mix
Spiced apple rings, for garnish

10 MIN.

1. Place pork roast in slow cooker and top with whole cranberries, reserving 1/2 cup. Pour in cranberry juice and add onions.
2. Sprinkle packet of dried onion soup mix over all.
3. Cook on Low for 8 hours and remove roast, onions, and cranberries to platter. Garnish with reserved fresh cranberries or spiced apple rings for additional color.

Serves 8 to10.

Drain as much grease as possible from stoneware insert as the roast nears the end of the cooking time. By then, much of the cranberry flavor will have penetrated the roast. If you prefer, garnish with spiced apple rings instead of cranberries, which tend to be bitter.

PORK ROAST

Leftovers can be great for busy days, but the trick is finding ways to make them look different. Combining slow-cooking technology with the advantage of quick and easy stir-fry cooking has led me to several interesting "Crock to Wok" recipes.

1 (3- to 4-lb.) Boston butt pork roast
Cracked black pepper, to taste
1 cup favorite barbecue sauce

5 MIN.

1. Place roast in slow cooker. Grind black pepper over roast. Turn to High for first hour of cooking and then to Low for 9 to 10 hours.
2. During the last 30 minutes of cooking time, drain off grease and pour barbecue sauce over roast. Cook for final 30 minutes on Low. Remove and slice.

Serves 8 to 10.

If you have a slow-cooker meat rack, this is a good time to use it.

 It is important to drain off grease near the end of cooking time, before adding barbecue sauce.

(See Crock to Wok pork recipe, page 74.)

CROCK TO WOK PORK ROAST SPECIAL

2 tbls. vegetable oil
1 medium onion, chopped
1 bag (1 lb. 5 ozs.) frozen stir-fry vegetables
1 1/2 cups cooked pork, diced
1 (3/4-oz.) package stir-fry Oriental seasoning mix
2 tbls. soy sauce
1 tsp. sugar
1/4 cup water
Cooked rice

15 MIN.

1. Heat oil in wok. Stir-fry onion, adding in frozen stir-fry vegetables. Cook for approximately 5 minutes, stirring constantly. Add in pork and cook until heated through.
2. Combine seasoning mix with soy sauce, sugar, and water. Add to wok mixture. Toss all together until well heated and serve over cooked rice.

Serves 4 to 6.

Frozen food manufacturers have several stir-fry meal packages to which you just add beef, poultry, or pork for a time-saving meal.

BARBECUE NEWMAN-STYLE

Try this in French or sub rolls and serve with cole slaw or potato salad. It's a casual meal that's sure to go great with a day of football games.

1 (3-lb.) bonesless pork roast
2 (14.5-oz.) cans stewed tomatoes
1 bunch celery, chopped
1 large onion, chopped
1 tbl. ground sage
Salt, pepper, or Konrico Greek seasoning, to taste
2 tbls. sugar
1 tbl. chili powder

PREP **TIME**
15 MIN.

1. Cook meat, tomatoes, and seasonings, except sugar and chili powder, until meat is tender enough to shred, approximately 8 hours on Low.
2. Remove meat and shred with a fork. Return meat to slow cooker. Add sugar and chili powder and mix well. Serve barbecue mixture on French or sub rolls, using slotted spoon.

Serves 8 to10.
Gloria Newman

For second version, use a 5-lb. rump roast instead of pork. One hour before serving, add 1 cup Masterpiece Original barbecue sauce. All other directions remain the same.

SLOW-COOKER BABY BACK RIBS

Most ribs are extremely tender when slow-cooked, making them a favorite for many slow-cooking enthusiasts.
A 5- to 6-quart oval cooker works best.

PREP TIME: 15 MIN.

1/4 cup Spicy Chili Mix, recipe follows
1/4 cup dark brown sugar
3 to 4 racks (1 lb. each) baby back ribs
1/2 cup favorite barbecue sauce or sweet and sour sauce

1. Mix spicy blend and brown sugar; rub on ribs. Curl racks, meaty side out; stand upright on thick ends in a 5- to 6-quart slow cooker.
2. Cover and cook on Low for 7 to 8 hours, or on High for 3 to 3 1/2 hours, or until meat is very tender.
3. Remove ribs to cutting board. Let rest for 5 minutes and brush with barbecue or sweet and sour sauce. Serve.

Serves 4 to 6.
Sandra Gwin

 SPEED SLOW Add onions or new potatoes to the center space, if desired.

SPICY CHILI MIX

1 tbl. ground black pepper
2 tsps. crushed red pepper flakes
2 tbls. chili powder
1 tbl. dark brown sugar
1 tbl. ground oregano
3 tbls. paprika
2 tbls. salt
1 tbl. granulated sugar

1. Mix and store in the refrigerator. Makes 1 cup.

ORIENTAL PORK

Those who enjoy pork will love the tender slow-cooked results from this dish.

4 to 5 boneless pork loin chops
1 (3/4-oz.) packet Oriental stir-fry seasoning mix
2 celery stalks, sliced
1 medium onion, cut into rings
1 tbl. soy sauce
1 (14-oz.) can chop suey vegetables, drained
1 (8-oz.) can sliced water chestnuts, drained
1 (8-oz.) can pineapple tidbits
1 bell pepper, sliced into strips

PREP TIME 10 MIN.

1. Place pork chops into slow cooker and cover with Oriental seasoning mix. Add in celery and onion, along with soy sauce.
2. Cook on Low for 6 to 7 hours.
3. Drain grease from stoneware insert and add in chop suey vegetables, water chestnuts, pineapple, and sliced bell pepper and cook for another hour. Serve over rice.

Serves 4 to 6.

 Don't forget to add a fortune cookie.

CORN-STUFFED PORK RIBS

Corn is one of those vegetables you can usually get children to eat. This recipe makes it especially tasty.

4 country-style pork ribs
1 tsp. cracked black pepper
4 cups frozen corn, partially thawed
2 (14 1/2-oz.) cans stewed tomatoes
1 tsp. sugar
1 green bell pepper, sliced (reserve some for garnish)
1 cup stale French bread cubes

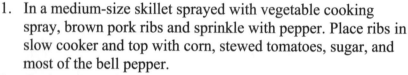

PREP TIME
15 MIN.

1. In a medium-size skillet sprayed with vegetable cooking spray, brown pork ribs and sprinkle with pepper. Place ribs in slow cooker and top with corn, stewed tomatoes, sugar, and most of the bell pepper.
2. Cook on Low for 8 hours. Using slotted spoon, remove ribs and corn/tomato mixture and put into oven-safe casserole dish. Top with bread pieces and place under broiler for a few minutes or until browned on top.

Serves 4.

UNDER
CONSTRUCTION

If you don't have stale French bread on hand, any type of bread will do.

APPLE-COVERED PORK CHOPS

Apple fans are sure to appreciate this recipe. Apple and pork make a great combination.

4 pork chops
1 onion, sliced in rings
1 Granny Smith apple, cored and sliced in rings
1/3 cup raisins
2 tbls. brown sugar
1 tbl. ground cinnamon
1/8 tsp. nutmeg
1/4 cup apple juice

PREP TIME

15 MIN.

1. In medium-size skillet, brown pork chops over medium-high heat. Drain off grease.
2. Place pork chops into slow cooker and top with onion, apple, and raisins. Mix brown sugar, cinnamon, and nutmeg together in a small bowl and sprinkle over pork chops. Pour apple juice around the sides of the stoneware insert and cook on Low for 6 to 8 hours.
3. Serve with wild rice.

Serves 4.

 SPEED SLOW   If you want an intense apple flavor, add more apple rings about an hour before cooking time is complete.

PORK AND SPAGHETTI SPECIAL

My family has always enjoyed spaghetti dishes of all kinds. Since I love pork, especially slowly cooked, this one was a keeper from the start.

4 country-style boneless pork strips, cut into
  cubes
2 tbls. vegetable oil
1 medium onion, chopped
1 green bell pepper, chopped
1 (26-oz.) can garlic and herb spaghetti sauce
1/4 tsp. dried ground oregano
1/4 tsp. Italian seasoning
1 tsp. ground black pepper
1 lb. thin spaghetti

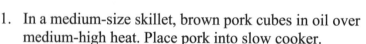

PREP   TIME

15 MIN.

1. In a medium-size skillet, brown pork cubes in oil over medium-high heat. Place pork into slow cooker.
2. Add onion, bell pepper, spaghetti sauce, and seasonings. Cook on Low for 6 to 8 hours.
3. Serve over cooked thin spaghetti.

Serves 4 to 6.

UNDER
CONSTRUCTION

There are many prepared spaghetti sauces on supermarket shelves. If you have a favorite, use it in place of the garlic and herb flavor. Feel free to substitute your own homemade variety, as well.

Soups & Stews

NO PEEP STEW

Mothers of toddlers will appreciate this one. It makes for an easy day in the kitchen, even if nothing else in your day is.

2 lbs. butterflied pork chops, cubed
1 (10 3/4-oz.) can reduced-fat cream of mushroom soup
1 (4-oz.) can mushrooms, stems and pieces, drained
1 (1-oz.) packet dried onion soup mix
1/2 cup red wine
Black pepper to taste
1/4 cup water
1 (l6-oz.) bag fresh baby carrots

PREP TIME 10 MIN.

1. Place all ingredients in slow cooker and cook on Low for 8 hours.
2. Serve over rice or noodles.

Serves 4 to 6.
Lee Anne Millard

If you prefer, lean stew meat can be used in place of the pork.

SAN ANTONIO STEW

San Antonio Stew is a natural for adapting to the slow-cooking method, as are most stews.

2 lbs. beef stew meat
1/4 cup all-purpose flour
1 tsp. Tony Chachere's Original Seasoning
1/4 cup vegetable oil
1 medium onion, coarsely chopped
2 cloves garlic, minced
1 tbl. dried parsley
1 tsp. ground cumin
1 (10 1/2-oz.) can beef broth
3/4 cup water
1 (8-oz.) jar chunky picante sauce
1 (15-oz.) can chopped tomatoes
1 (16-oz.) bag fresh baby carrots
2 zucchini, cut into 1-inch pieces
2 cups frozen corn kernels

PREP TIME

15 MIN.

1. Shake stew meat in bag with flour and Tony Chachere's.
2. In a skillet, brown meat in 1/4 cup hot oil. Add onion and garlic and sauté over medium heat.
3. Place beef mixture into slow cooker and add seasonings, broth, water, picante sauce, tomatoes, carrots, zucchini, and corn.
4. Cook on Low for 6 to 8 hours.

Serves 6 to 8.
Connie Caldwell

TOSTADA TEX-MEX SOUP

Soups are especially delightful when prepared in the slow cooker. This one is relatively easy, and the spices merge throughout the day, creating a meal worth coming home to.

1 lb. ground sirloin
1 onion, chopped
1 (14 1/2-oz.) can zesty diced tomatoes with jalapeño peppers
1 (16-oz.) can pinto beans, drained
1 (8-oz.) can tomato sauce
1 1/2 cups water
3/4 cup chunky picante sauce
Crushed tortilla chips
Monterey Jack cheese, shredded

PREP TIME

15 MIN.

1. Cook sirloin with onion in a skillet over medium-high heat and drain before placing in slow cooker.
2. Add all other ingredients, except crushed chips and cheese, and stir. Cook on Low for 8 hours and spoon into individual soup bowls. Top with crushed tortilla chips and shredded Monterey Jack cheese.

Serves 4 to 6.

This might be a bit too spicy for some youngsters. If desired, you can substitute the regular diced tomatoes for the zesty ones.

SLOW LENTIL SOUP

You can't beat this soup on a cold winter's day, and, yes, it's good on warm days, too. Either way, chili, soups, and stews are family pleasers year-round.

4 cups lentils, rinsed and sorted
1 onion, chopped
2 links smoked sausage, sliced
1 (10-oz.) can Ro-tel tomatoes
1 (8-oz.) can tomato sauce
1 (4-oz.) can tomato paste
2 cloves garlic, minced
1 tsp. salt
1 tsp. black pepper
6 cups water
Chopped green onions, optional

1. Place all ingredients, except green onions, into slow cooker and cook on Low for 8 hours. Ladle into bowls and garnish with chopped green onions, if desired.

Serves 6 to 8.

 Serve with French bread or Texas toast and a green salad to round out the meal.

PEPPERONI PASTA SOUP

This is perfect for lunch or a light dinner selection.

2 (10 3/4-oz.) cans Italian tomato soup with basil and oregano
1 (14.5-oz.) can stewed tomatoes, undrained
2 cups water
1/4 cup tri-colored rotini pasta
1 (3.5-oz.) package sliced pepperoni
1/2 cup herb-seasoned croutons
1/4 cup shredded mozzarella and Cheddar cheese,
  blended

PREP TIME

10 MIN.

1. Place all ingredients, except croutons and cheese, in slow cooker. Cook on Low for 4 to 6 hours.
2. Place croutons in the bottom of four soup bowls and top with soup. Sprinkle cheese on top. Some may choose to add more cheese.

Serves 4.

SHRIMP AND CORN SOUP

Soups are great to come home to whatever the season, but I admit, on those cold, damp days, it doesn't get much better than this.

2 (15 1/4-oz.) cans cream-style corn
1 (15 1/4-oz.) can whole-kernel corn, drained
1 (10-oz.) can Ro-tel tomatoes
1/2 bell pepper, chopped
1 onion, chopped
2 cloves garlic, minced
1/4 cup chopped parsley
1 (8-oz.) can tomato sauce
2 stalks celery, chopped
4 cups water
1 (10 3/4-oz.) can cream of celery soup
2 tbls. Worcestershire sauce
Tony Chachere's Original Seasoning, to taste
1 1/2 lbs. shrimp, peeled
1 bunch green onions, chopped

PREP TIME 15 MIN.

1. Place all ingredients into slow cooker, except shrimp and green onions. Cook on Low for 8 hours. Add shrimp during last hour of cooking. Stir and turn cooker to High.
2. Ladle into bowls and garnish with green onions.

Serves 6.

Peeling the shrimp takes extra prep time, so allow for that on this one.

JALAPEÑO STEW

Jalapeños are basic to many favorite dishes, just as stews are favorites for slow-cooker fans. Combining the two makes for a wonderful marriage.

2 lbs. round steak, cut into cubes
All-purpose flour
2 tbls. vegetable oil
1/2 cup water
1 (14 1/2-oz.) can zesty diced tomatoes with jalapeño peppers
1 (15-oz.) can whole-kernel corn
1 (15-oz.) can diced carrots
1 (15-oz.) can mixed vegetables
1 (10 1/2-oz.) can onion-seasoned beef broth
1 (1-oz.) packet dried onion soup mix

1. Place round steak in plastic container or bag and shake with enough flour to cover.
2. In a skillet, brown steak in vegetable oil over medium-high heat and add water. Turn to low heat and simmer for 15 minutes.
3. Place round steak and gravy into slow cooker and pour all other ingredients over beef. Cook on Low for 8 hours.

Serves 8 to 10.

BLACK BEAN CHILI LOUISIANE

One of those winter favorites, chili is perfect to come home to on a cold day. The simmering flavors make this one a winner.

1 tbl. olive oil
1 onion, chopped
1 bell pepper, chopped
3 cloves garlic, minced
1 tbl. chili powder
1/4 tsp. crushed red pepper flakes
1 (28-oz.) can diced tomatoes
2 (15-oz.) cans black beans, rinsed and drained
1 (4-oz.) can chopped green chilies, drained
Feta cheese, crumbled

PREP TIME
15 MIN.

1. In a skillet, cook onion, bell pepper, and garlic in olive oil over medium-high heat.
2. Sprinkle chili powder and crushed pepper flakes over mixture and cook until onion and bell pepper are slightly roasted, about 4 to 5 minutes.
3. Transfer vegetables to slow cooker and add in all remaining ingredients, except cheese. Cook on Low for 8 hours.
4. Ladle into bowls and top with feta cheese.

Serves 4 to 6.

HOT-SAUCED CHILI

The introduction of convenience sauces has made slow cooking easier than ever. I'm a big proponent of checking supermarket shelves for the latest products. How's this one for convenience?

1 lb. ground sirloin
1 onion, chopped
2 stalks celery, chopped
1 (16-oz.) jar Tabasco's 7-Spice chili sauce
2 cups water
1 (15-oz.) can cannellini beans, undrained
Monterey Jack cheese

15 MIN.

1. In a skillet, brown ground sirloin with onion over medium-high heat and drain.
2. Transfer beef and onion to slow cooker and add remaining ingredients, except cheese. Cook on Low for 6 to 8 hours and ladle into bowls.
3. Top with Monterey Jack cheese.

Serves 6 to 8.

 Jalapeño cornbread is a great addition to this meal.

WHITE BEAN FIESTA STEW

On those cold days -- and, yes, we do have them in the South -- a nice simmering stew is great comfort food.

1 lb. dried white beans
3/4 cup lentils
1 tsp. salt
1 tsp. ground black pepper
4 cups water
2 cloves garlic, minced
3 links andouille sausage, sliced
1 medium onion, chopped
3 stalks celery, chopped
1 (10-oz.) can Ro-tel tomatoes
Chopped green onions for garnish, optional

PREP TIME

15 MIN.

1. Soak white beans overnight. Drain and place in slow cooker; add lentils, salt, pepper, water, garlic, sausage, onions, celery, and tomatoes.
2. Cook on Low for 8 hours. Ladle into individual soup bowls and garnish with chopped green onions.

Serves 4 to 6.

Serve with French bread and salad.
If you are unable to locate andouille, use smoked sausage as a substitute.

TURNIP GREEN SOUP

Even those who aren't turnip green fans will like this soup.

1/3 of a 16-oz. bag of dried baby lima beans
8 cups water
6 small turnips with the greens
3 strips bacon
2 medium onions, chopped
1/2 cup slivered tasso
1 1/2 cups chopped or slivered ham
Salt and pepper, to taste

1. In a saucepan, cover beans with water and bring to a boil on stove top. Turn off heat and let sit for an hour. Drain.
2. Put drained beans in slow cooker with 8 cups water.
3. Peel and chop turnips and greens into bite-size pieces and place in slow cooker. In a skillet, fry bacon and put into slow cooker. Sauté onions in bacon drippings until limp, but not brown. Add to slow cooker.
4. Add tasso and ham. Cook on High for about 5 hours or until beans are tender. Add salt and pepper to taste.

Serves 8.
Lynn Roberts

 Use a 6-quart slow cooker for this one.
Baby lima beans work best for this recipe.

GOOD OLD-FASHIONED CHICKEN SOUP

When a cold or the flu sets in, there's nothing like a simmering pot of chicken soup.

3 large skinless chicken breast halves, bone in
5 cups chicken broth
2 stalks celery, chopped
1 large onion, chopped
3 carrots, sliced thin
1 (10 3/4-oz.) can stewed tomatoes
3 small red potatoes, diced
1 cup fresh green beans
2 cloves garlic, minced
1 tsp. salt
1 tsp. black pepper
1 tsp. Tabasco sauce

15 MIN.

1. Place chicken into slow cooker and add all other ingredients. Stir and cook on Low for 6 to 8 hours.
2. One hour before cooking time is complete, remove chicken breasts with slotted spoon and gently pull chicken off the bone. Return chicken meat to the soup. Continue to cook soup for the remaining hour.

Serves 4 to 6.

Whenever you are boiling chicken on your stove top for any recipe, be sure to save the broth. Freeze in small freezer containers for use in recipes such as the one above. Canned or fresh broth can be used for this soup.

POTATO-ASPARAGUS SOUP

This is a nice choice for a luncheon or light dinner.

6 medium potatoes, peeled and finely chopped
2 (14 1/2-oz.) cans garlic-flavored chicken broth
1 small onion, chopped
1 (14 1/2-oz.) can asparagus, drained
1 1/2 cups half-and-half
1/4 cup all-purpose flour
1 tsp. black pepper

PREP   TIME

15 MIN.

1. Place potatoes into slow cooker. Add chicken broth, onion, and asparagus and cook on High for 4 hours.
2. Mix half-and-half and flour well, and pour into slow cooker. Sprinkle on black pepper and cook on Low for an additional 2 hours.
3. Ladle into soup bowls and serve.

Serves 4.

If you decide to use fresh asparagus, precook before placing in slow cooker.

Louisiana Favorites

RED BEANS AND RICE

Nothing says Louisiana better than Red Beans and Rice.

1 lb. dried red kidney beans
1 cup cooked ham pieces
1 (14 1/2-oz.) can zesty diced tomatoes with
   jalapeño peppers
1 onion, chopped
1 tbl. Worcestershire sauce
1 tsp. Tabasco sauce
2 bay leaves
2 cloves garlic, minced
4 tbls. chopped parsley
6 cups water
Hot, cooked rice

1. Soak red beans overnight in enough water to cover beans.
2. Drain beans and place in slow cooker. Add in ham, tomatoes, onions, and all other seasonings. Pour water over all and cook on Low for 6 to 8 hours or until beans are tender.
3. Serve over rice.

Serves 4 to 6.

Soak dried beans overnight before putting them in the slow cooker. Drain the water off the following morning before placing them in the cooker. Replace with 6 cups fresh water for the cooking process.

SHRIMP CREOLE

Slow cooking can be Cajun. Make a roux and try your hand at one of my favorites, Shrimp Creole. Use a 5- to 6-quart cooker.

QUICK ROUX

2/3 cup oil
2/3 cup all-purpose flour
1 cup chopped onion
1 cup chopped celery
1/4 cup chopped green bell pepper
3 cloves garlic, minced
1/4 cup chopped parsley
1/4 cup green onion tops
1 cup hot water

PREP TIME
15 MIN.

1. Mix oil and flour together and microwave 6-7 minutes. Stir at the end of 6 minutes. Add onion, celery, bell pepper, garlic, parsley, and green onion. Stir and place back in microwave.
2. Sauté on High for 5 minutes and add 1 cup hot water. Stir and put in cooker.

SHRIMP CREOLE

1 (28-oz.) can diced tomatoes
1 (8-oz.) can tomato sauce
1 (6-oz.) can tomato paste
1 tbl. Tony Chachere's Original Seasoning
1 tsp. Tabasco sauce
1 1/2 to 2 lbs. raw, peeled shrimp

1. After placing roux into slow cooker, add tomato products, seasoning, and Tabasco. Cook on Low for 7 hours.
2. Turn slow cooker to High and add shrimp. Cook for another hour and 30 minutes. Serve over rice.

Serves 6 to 8.

REDFISH COURTBOUILLON

Here in the Bayou State, the catch of the day is varied. In our household, redfish is prized and deserves special treatment. Over the years, courtbouillon has been served on many special occasions. Hope you enjoy it as much as we do.

1 lb. redfish or red snapper fillets
3 tbls. Tony Chachere's Original Seasoning
2 tbls. teriyaki sauce
1 tbl. Tabasco sauce
1 tbl. lemon juice
1 large onion, chopped
4 ribs celery, chopped
1/2 green bell pepper, chopped
1 (28-oz.) can diced tomatoes
2 (6-oz.) cans tomato paste
2 (8-oz.) cans tomato sauce
1 cup water
Black pepper, to taste

PREP TIME 15 MIN.

1. In a small bowl, mix Tony Chachere's, teriyaki sauce, Tabasco sauce, and lemon juice. Pour over fillets and marinate overnight.
2. Place onions, celery, bell pepper, diced tomatoes, tomato paste, tomato sauce, and water into slow cooker, mixing well. Sprinkle with black pepper.
3. Cook on Low for 8 to 10 hours. During last hour and a half of cooking time, turn to High and add fish and marinade. Stir well before replacing lid.
4. When fish flakes easily, the courtbouillon is ready to eat.
5. Serve over hot rice.

Serves 6 to 8.

This makes an impressive dish when entertaining.

CAJUN LIMAS

Beans are an integral ingredient in several Louisiana favorites.
Here's one to try Louisiana-style.

1 lb. dried baby lima beans
1 lb. andouille sausage
1 bunch green onions, chopped
1 tbl. cracked black pepper
3 vegetable broth cubes
1 tsp. Tabasco sauce
1 clove garlic, minced
4 cups water

1. Soak lima beans overnight. Drain and place beans in slow cooker.
2. Cut andouille into slices and add to cooker with all other seasonings. Pour 4 cups fresh water over all.
3. Cook on Low for 6 to 8 hours.

Serves 6 to 8.

If you are unable to locate andouille, use smoked sausage and add 1 teaspoon crushed red pepper flakes.

SLOW SWEET POTATO CASSEROLE

Sweet potatoes are a menu staple in Louisiana and in many households across the country just about year-round. Enjoy this slow-cooked version.

**2 (29-oz.) cans sweet potatoes or 4 to 6 cups fresh, peeled and
  cooked sweet potatoes
1/2 cup milk
5 tbls. butter
1/4 cup freshly grated coconut
1 tbl. grated orange peel
1/2 tsp. cinnamon
1/2 tsp. nutmeg
5 eggs, beaten
1/2 cup brown sugar
1/2 cup chopped pecans**

PREP TIME 15 MIN.

1. In large bowl of electric mixer, beat sweet potatoes, milk, and butter.
2. Fold in coconut, orange peel, cinnamon, nutmeg, and eggs.
3. Spray sides and bottom of slow cooker with vegetable cooking spray and pour in mixture.
4. Cover and cook on High for 2 hours, then turn to Low for another 2 hours.
5. In a small bowl, mix together brown sugar and pecans and sprinkle over cooked casserole. Cover and allow heat to steam sugar/pecan topping.

Serves 6 to 8.

MARDI GRAS WHITE BEANS

There's a lot to enjoy when it comes to Louisiana foods. Try slow cooking with Louisiana flair.

1 (14-oz.)package Cajun white beans with seasonings
1 medium onion, chopped
1 bell pepper, chopped
1/4 lb. pork tasso, sliced
6 cups water

PREP TIME

10 MIN.

1. Soak beans overnight in enough water to cover. In the morning, drain and place beans, onion, bell pepper, seasoning packet, and pork tasso in slow cooker.
2. Pour in enough water to cover beans, about 6 cups should do it. Cook on Low for 6 to 8 hours or until beans are soft.

Serves 6 to 8.
Laura Russell

If you can't find the Cajun white beans convenience package in your area, use an equivalent amount of any dried white beans and season with Tony Chachere's Original Seasoning and crushed red pepper flakes to taste.Tasso may be hard to find outside of Louisiana. Substitute smoked sausage, if necessary.

VENISON SALSA

In Louisiana, hunting is more than fair game, it's a slow-cooking opportunity. You can't miss with this one -- just two ingredients!

1 (4-lb.) venison roast
1 (32-oz.) jar Pace picante sauce, chunky
or traditional

5 MIN.

1. Place venison in slow cooker and cover with 3/4 of sauce in jar, reserving remaining amount.
2. Cook on Low for 8 to10 hours.
3. Remove roast from slow cooker and slice thinly. Pour remaining picante sauce over venison slices.

Serves 6 to 8.
George Rupert

If you do not have a hunter in your family, a good chuck or rump roast substitutes nicely.

VENISON CHILI

Venison is a popular dish in Louisiana, and just about any hunter has a favorite venison recipe. Adapting them to slow cooking is easy.

1 lb. ground venison
1 onion, chopped
1 bell pepper, chopped
3 garlic cloves, minced
2 tsps. chili powder
4 tbls. Worcestershire sauce
1 (8-oz.) can tomato sauce
2 (6-oz.) cans tomato paste
4 cups water
2 jalapeño peppers, diced
1 (16-oz.) can dark red kidney beans
Cheddar cheese, optional

PREP TIME
15 MIN.

1. In a skillet, brown ground venison with onion over medium-high heat and transfer to slow cooker.
2. Add all other ingredients, except cheese, and cook on Low for 6 to 8 hours. Ladle into bowls and top with Cheddar cheese.

Serves 6 to 8.

If you do not have venison in your freezer, substitute lean ground beef or ground turkey.

GOOSE MACALUSO STYLE

Venison and speckled-belly geese are especially well-suited to the long hours of slow cooking.

1 speckled-belly goose or 2 Cornish hens
Scant amount vegetable oil
1 small onion, chopped
3 cloves garlic, minced
1 green bell pepper, chopped
1 (16-oz.) package fresh baby carrots
White or rosé wine, enough to cover 3/4 inch on stoneware
  insert floor
Salt and white, red, or cayenne pepper to taste
1 (1-oz.) packet dried onion soup mix

PREP TIME 15 MIN.

1. In Dutch oven, brown goose or Cornish hens in small amount of oil. Remove goose or hens and sauté onion, garlic, and bell pepper in remaining juices over medium-high heat.
2. Place goose or hens, breast side down, in slow cooker and add carrots, sautéed vegetables, wine, and seasonings. Sprinkle dried onion soup mix on top.
3. Cook on Low for 8 hours and serve with rice.

Serves 4.
Joe Macaluso

 When cooking ducks or geese in the slow cooker, the key is to brown them well first in order to remove the fatty layer stored underneath the skin. Browning should include the standard seasonings of onion, garlic, bell pepper, and any other flavor you desire in a small amount of oil.

Use a 6-quart slow cooker if you will be cooking a goose. The goose may need to be cut into pieces in order to fit.

APPLE BREAD PUDDING

This is an old family favorite. The only big decision is choosing between whipped cream or vanilla ice cream.

9 Granny Smith apples, peeled and chopped
1/2 cup margarine
1 cup brown sugar
1/2 loaf French bread
Dash salt
1/4 cup orange juice
1 1/2 tsps. cinnamon
1/4 tsp. nutmeg
Whipped cream or vanilla ice cream, if desired

PREP TIME 15 MIN.

1. Place apples in slow cooker. Put margarine in small, microwavable bowl and heat for about 25 to 30 seconds on High, or until melted. Stir brown sugar into margarine.
2. Crumble French bread and place on top of apples.
3. Pour margarine/sugar mixture over apples and bread. Add in salt and orange juice. Sprinkle cinnamon and nutmeg over all.
4. Set slow cooker on Low and cook for 4 to 6 hours or until apples test done, but not mushy. Serve with ice cream or whipped cream.

Serves 6.
Millie Parmenter

 REDUCE SPEED Chopping apples takes a few extra minutes of time, so allow for that in your schedule.

WARM FRUIT CIDER

Ciders are popular beverages in the slow cooker. The warm simmering flavors not only take the chill off, but add wonderful aromas to your home.

1 (64-oz.) bottle apple cider
2 oranges, cut into quarters, peeled
2 lemons, cut into slices, with peel
6 whole cloves
4 cinnamon sticks

5 MIN.

1. Pour apple cider in slow cooker and add all remaining ingredients.
2. Cook on Low for 3 to 4 hours. When ready to serve, remove orange quarters, lemons, whole cloves, and cinnamon sticks.
3. Pour into individual mugs or punch cups and serve.

Serves 10 to 12.

You may place a cinnamon stick into each cup for garnish if desired.

GOBLIN MIX

Try this snack for Halloween parties and after-school treats. Use a 5- to 6-quart slow cooker.

2 cups mini-twisted pretzels
3 cups rice Chex cereal
2 cups Kix cereal
1 cup salted cashews
1 cup goldfish crackers
1/2 cup margarine, melted
1/8 cup Worcestershire sauce
1 tbl. garlic powder
1 tsp. cayenne pepper

5 MIN.

1. Mix pretzels, Chex cereal, Kix cereal, cashews, and crackers in slow cooker.
2. In microwavable bowl, melt margarine over low heat and stir in Worcestershire sauce, garlic powder, and cayenne pepper.
3. Pour melted margarine and seasonings over dry mixture in the slow cooker, cover, and cook on Low for 3 to 4 hours. Uncover for the last 45 minutes.

Serves 12 to 15.

 Let cool completely before storing in plastic storage containers or bags.

MORNING QUESADILLAS

Our family has found that sports events can take over a weekend. If you're lucky enough to have a couple of hours to prepare breakfast before a big game, try this in your slow cooker.

3/4 cup diced cooked ham
1/3 cup chopped fresh Roma tomatoes
1/4 cup chopped green onions
1 tbl. hot sauce
1 cup shredded Monterey Jack cheese
1 cup shredded Cheddar cheese
4 to 6 flour tortillas
2 tbls. butter

1. Place ham, tomatoes, and green onions in slow cooker. Sprinkle in hot sauce and cook on Low for 2 hours.
2. Fold in cheeses and cook for 10 minutes or until cheese is completely melted.
3. In a skillet, lightly brown tortillas in 2 tablespoons of butter over medium heat. Put a small amount of filling in each tortilla, then roll up and garnish with more cheese and green onion, if desired.

Serves 4 to 6.

 This is a quick recipe that can either be served at a brunch or enjoyed by the family before weekend activities begin in earnest.

SPICED TEA SOUTHERN-STYLE

If you're having a luncheon, a flavored tea is a great addition to finger sandwiches and cookies.

6 cups boiling water
2 black tea bags
2 cinnamon sticks
1 cup orange juice
1/4 cup fresh lemon juice
1/2 cup sugar

PREP TIME

10 MIN.

1. Pour boiling water over tea bags and cinnamon in slow cooker. Let tea steep for 30 minutes.
2. Add remaining ingredients and cook on Low for 3 to 4 hours. Remove tea bags and cinnamon sticks and serve.

Serves 6 to 8.

This tea stays warm as long as your slow cooker remains on. The attractive designs in today's slow cookers make a pretty addition to a buffet table.

WARM SAUCE

Holidays are wonderful times to use the slow cooker. Enjoy this sauce for those special meals.

**2 (16-oz.) cans whole-berry
    cranberry sauce
2 (6-oz.) cans crushed pineapple, drained
2 tsps. lemon juice**

5 MIN.

1. Stir all ingredients together in slow cooker and cook on Low for 4 to 6 hours.
2. Serve warm over cold leftover chicken, ham, or turkey or over warm meats or poultry.

Serves 4 to 6.
Jewell Crum

This is a perfect accompaniment for turkey, whether warm from the oven or left over.

VEGGIE PASTA

1/2 cup dried chick peas or garbanzo beans
1/2 cup dried navy beans
1/2 cup dried red kidney beans
4 cups water
2 cups grated carrots
1/2 cup each of sliced celery and chopped green bell pepper
2 cloves garlic, minced
1/2 cup chopped onion
1 (10-oz.) can Ro-tel tomatoes
1 (14 1/2-oz.) can stewed tomatoes, mashed   **15 MIN.**
2 (15-oz.) cans Contadina thick and zesty
  tomato sauce
2 cups fresh mushrooms, sliced
1/4 tsp. basil
1/4 tsp. ground oregano
1 tsp. Tony Chachere's Original Seasoning
1 1/2 tbls. chili powder (use more if desired)
1 (10-oz.) package yolk-free noodles
Butter-flavored nonfat vegetable spray
1 1/2 cups Kraft fat-free shredded sharp cheese
Fat-free Parmesan cheese, to taste

1. Place all peas and beans and water in a 5- to 6-quart slow
   cooker. Cook on Low overnight, 8 to 10 hours.
2. In the morning, add carrots, celery, green pepper, garlic,
   onion, tomato products, mushrooms, and seasonings.
3. Cook on Low about 12 hours. Shortly before serving, cook
   noodles; drain and spray with butter-flavored spray, then
   place noodles in a 9x13x2-inch baking dish and sprinkle
   shredded sharp cheese on top. Pour bean/vegetable mixture
   over all and mix. Sprinkle Parmesan cheese on top.

Serves 8 to 10.
Andy Roberts

ITALIAN POTATOES

Your family will flip over this recipe. Serve with cube steaks and salad for a special meal.

6 large potatoes, sliced in rounds
1 onion, sliced
4 ozs. sliced pepperoni
1 green bell pepper, sliced in strips
Cracked black pepper
Ground oregano, to taste
Italian seasoning, to taste
1 (28-oz.) jar pizza, spaghetti, or pasta sauce
Cheddar cheese or pizza cheese blend, shredded

1. Slice potatoes and layer with onion, pepperoni, bell pepper, black pepper, oregano, Italian seasoning, and pizza sauce.
2. Continue layering until all ingredients are used. Cook on Low for 6 to 8 hours.
3. Sprinkle with shredded Cheddar or pizza cheese blend.

Serves 4 to 6.

 This is an extremely "children-friendly" recipe. Let them take part in sprinkling seasonings and pouring sauce. The more they participate, the more likely they are to enjoy their food, although this recipe probably won't require much persuasion.

ONIONS, SLOW-COOKED STYLE

Onion lovers are sure to give this one a thumbs up. Even those who don't care for onions will be surprised by the sweet flavor when they are prepared in the slow cooker.

5 large onions, yellow or white
1/2 cup butter

5 MIN.

1. Wash and peel onions and slice into rings or cubes, depending on personal preference. Place in slow cooker and add butter.
2. Cover and cook on Low for 8 hours.

Serves 5.
Laurie Smith Anderson

 Use this as a side dish for any number of entrees or add to soups and stews. If there are leftovers, refrigerate and add to dinner menus over the following days.

If Vidalia onions are available, they make a good choice for this recipe.

NEW POTATO FALL FARE

Be creative with your potatoes. Try an artistic zigzag design in the process to create a special look.

8 to 10 new potatoes (small red potatoes)   **15 MIN.**
1 (16-oz.) package fresh baby carrots
1 medium onion, chopped
1 (14.5-oz.) can chicken broth, preferably garlic flavored
1/4 cup chopped parsley

1. Make a zigzag design on the skin of the potatoes with a potato peeler.
2. Place potatoes in slow cooker and add carrots and onions. Pour chicken broth over all.
3. Cook on Low for 6 to 8 hours. During last 10 minutes of cooking time, add in parsley.
4. Remove vegetables with slotted spoon and serve.

Serves 6 to 8.

Reserve some fresh parsley for garnish at the end. Want to add some spice? Add a dash of Creole seasoning or cayenne pepper.

VEGETABLE MEDLEY

Squash and zucchini do well in the slow cooker.

5 zucchini, sliced thick
1 lb. fresh mushrooms, whole
1 onion, chopped
1 green bell pepper, chopped
1 tsp. black pepper
1/2 tsp. ground oregano
1/2 tsp. Italian seasoning
1 (15-oz.) can stewed tomatoes
1 (8-oz.) package shredded mozzarella cheese

10 MIN.

1. Place zucchini, mushrooms, onion, and bell pepper into slow cooker.
2. Sprinkle seasonings over all and pour stewed tomatoes on top.
3. Cook on Low for 6 hours, adding in cheese during the last 10 minutes.

Serves 4 to 6.

Children often need to be persuaded to eat their veggies. The cheese may convince them to give this one a try.

PINEAPPLE LAGNIAPPE

It always adds to the meal when you have a bit of "sweetness" on the side.

1 (6-oz.) package zwieback crackers, crumbled
1 (6-oz.) can crushed pineapple, drained
1/2 cup butter, melted

1. Crumble zwieback into bottom of stoneware insert. Add pineapple and pour melted butter over all.
2. Cook on Low for 4 hours and serve as a side dish with ham.

Serves 4 to 6.

 Lagniappe is a favorite term in Louisiana, meaning "a little something extra." This definitely qualifies.

MARTIN'S ALL-DAY BEANS

When Lowery Martin makes this recipe for his mother's church, he leaves out the bourbon. While it gives the beans a caramel flavor, it may be left out.

2 (16-oz.) cans Bush's original baked beans
1 tsp. dry mustard
1/2 cup bottled chili sauce
2 tbls. molasses (country-style)
1/4 cup strong coffee
1 (16-oz.) can pineapple chunks, drained
2 tbls. dark brown sugar
1/4 cup bourbon

10 MIN.

1. Mix all ingredients in slow cooker and cook on Low for 8 hours.
2. Steam off excess liquid during the last hour by leaving cooker uncovered.

Serves 8 to 10.
Lowery L. Martin

This recipe can easily be doubled if you need a larger quantity.

SHRIMP DIP

Dips are wonderfully easy in the slow cooker, and best of all, they require little attention.

1 (8-oz.) package cream cheese
1 (10 3/4-oz.) can cream of shrimp soup
1 bunch green onions, chopped
1/2 tsp. Tabasco sauce
1 tbl. Worcestershire sauce

10 MIN.

1. Cut cream cheese into cubes and mix with soup in slow cooker. Cook mixture on Low for 2 hours.
2. Add onions and Tabasco and Worcestershire sauces; stir and continue cooking for another 2 hours on Low.
3. Serve with your choice of crackers or chips.

Serves 6 to 8.

This is one dish where stirring halfway through is especially important in order to ensure a creamy and thoroughly mixed dip.

PENNY'S SPICED PECANS

This is a quick and easy entertaining special.

1 (1-lb.) package shelled pecan halves
1/4 cup butter or margarine
3 tbls. Tony Chachere's Original Seasoning

1. Place pecans in slow cooker. In a small microwavable bowl, melt margarine or butter and pour over pecans.
2. Sprinkle 1 1/2 tablespoons of seasoning over all and stir. Sprinkle remaining seasoning over top of nuts and cook on High for 1 1/2 hours. Remove cover and turn cooker to Low for an additional 45 minutes, stirring once halfway through.
3. Remove pecans from cooker and spread on wax paper until nuts cool completely and serve.

Makes 1 pound.
Debbie Penny

BAKED GRANOLA APPLES

Apples and granola are an appealing combination, especially when a fresh crop of apples has just arrived at your local produce market.

**4 Golden Delicious or Granny Smith
  apples
1 1/2 cups granola cereal
1/4 cup raisins
3 tbls. ground cinnamon
3 tbls. sugar
1/2 cup butter or margarine, melted
Whipped topping or vanilla ice cream**

15 MIN.

1. Core apples almost to bottom and cut enough apple away from core area to make a good "well" in the center.
2. Place apples in slow cooker and spoon enough granola cereal into each apple to almost fill the "well." Finish filling the "well" with a tablespoon of raisins.
3. Mix ground cinnamon and sugar together and sprinkle over filling in apples. Drizzle melted butter or margarine over filling. Cook on Low for 3 to 4 hours. Remove and immediately top with whipped topping or vanilla ice cream.

Serves 4.

SLOW HOPPIN' JOHN

Here in the South, Hoppin' John is a favorite, especially around New Year's.

1 lb. dried black-eyed peas, rinsed and sorted
1 onion, chopped
3 stalks celery, chopped
3 garlic cloves, minced
5 cups water
1 (14 1/2-oz.) can beef broth
4 slices uncooked bacon, cut in half
1 tsp. crushed red pepper flakes
Hot, cooked rice

PREP TIME

15 MIN.

1. In a large pot, put peas and enough water to cover. Soak overnight.
2. The next morning, drain water off and put peas into slow cooker with onion, celery, garlic, water, beef broth, bacon, and red pepper. Cook on Low for 8 hours.
3. Just before cooking time is complete, cook rice in a separate pot. Set aside until peas are ready. Serve peas over rice.

Serves 8.

UNDER CONSTRUCTION

For those who enjoy Hoppin' John with more salt, add a teaspoon of salt when you put all ingredients into the cooker.

TOP TEN TIME-SAVER TIPS

1. If chopped onions, celery, or bell pepper is called for, chop the night before. Store in sandwich bags in the refrigerator.

2. Locate all spices and canned ingredients that the recipe calls for the night before and place on the kitchen counter where you can easily find them in the morning.

3. Have the cookbook or recipe where you can't miss it. The last thing you want to do is look for a missing recipe while you're trying to make lunches, get to work, or make it on time to a morning appointment.

4. If a recipe calls for cutting meat into cubes or strips, do that the night before and refrigerate until ready to place in the cooker.

5. It will save you a great deal of time and aggravation if you routinely make certain to check that the slow cooker is plugged in, turned on, and getting warm before you leave the house.

6. Plan ahead. Remember, planning saves time in the long run.

7. Spray stoneware insert with a light coating of vegetable cooking spray to make cleanup easier.

8. Use convenience sauces and mixes whenever possible.

9. When food is cooked, serve directly from removable insert, rather than other serving bowls, to eliminate extra dishes to be washed.

10. If you're making a casserole or spaghetti sauce, make a double batch if your slow cooker is large enough and freeze one for use another day.

ORDER FORM
Fast Lane Productions, L.L.C.
P.O. Box 87527 Baton Rouge, LA 70879-8527

Please send _____ copies of Slow Cookin' in the Fast Lane
@ $16.95 each $_____
  Plus postage and handling @ 2.95 each $_____
  Louisiana residents add 8% sales tax $_____
                Total $_____

Name:_____

Address:_____

City/State/ZIP:_____

_____

Make checks payable to: Fast Lane Productions, L.L.C.

==

ORDER FORM
Fast Lane Productions, L.L.C.
P.O. Box 87527 Baton Rouge, LA 70879-8527

Please send _____ copies of Slow Cookin' in the Fast Lane
@ $16.95 each $_____
  Plus postage and handling @ 2.95 each $_____
  Louisiana residents add 8% sales tax   Tax $_____
              Total $_____

Name:_____

Address:_____

City/State/ZIP:_____

_____

Make checks payable to: Fast Lane Productions, L.L.C.